The Ancient H

GW01003376

God

and

Anti-Gods

Through Agamas and Vedic Traditions

L. H. Reddy

The Ancient History of Gods and Anti-Gods: through Agamas and Vedic Traditions

ISBN-13: 978-1545506141

ISBN-10: 1545506140

Library of Congress Control Number: 2017906550
CreateSpace Independent Publishing Platform, North Charleston, SC

Front Cover Page: Statue of Goddess Saraswati (Goddess of Knowledge) situated on the Banks of Godavari River, Basar Village, Telangana, India. The original statue was built by Sage Veda Vyas immediately after Mahabharata war, more than five thousand years ago, that was the beginning of idol worship in Ancient India.

Inner Cover Page: Shore Temple, Mahabalipuram, India; 8th century CE, a replica of ancient flying machines.

Dedication

To my parents in Heaven (my mother Late Bhudevi Reddy, who taught me Ramayana, Mahabharata and Vaishnavite traditions when I was a child and my father Late L. Laxmi Kanth Reddy, who was my best friend and who taught me history of my ancestors).

And to my wife (Samyuktha), my daughter (Waghmini), my brothers (L. Srinivas Reddy, L. V. Ramana Reddy and L.V. Narasimha Reddy), my sister (M. Venkata Ramani Reddy) and my brother-in-law (M. Ashok Reddy).

Table of Contents

Section - V

(Definition of God)

Preface

This title is a concise history of the ancient Vedic Gods along with the historical accounts of Puranic Gods and Asuras. People oftentimes think Anti-Gods or Asuras are the rulers of South. This is certainly true during the Puranic period, but it may not be the case with the Vedic era. Indo-Aryans played a central role in safeguarding the Vedas which they accumulated it from the Dravidian clan - Kshatriyas, even though Vedic culture began long before their arrival.

There is a lot of controversy surrounding the exact dateline of Vedic people? Chapter-1 discusses about the early Vedic gods and the chronology of the ancient Indian civilization. Astronomy was the key element in advancement of Vedic society. Chapter-2 provides the fundamentals of Vedic Astronomy and Vedic Calendar.

Mahabharata was the last time when Gods, Asuras and Men roamed together the planet Earth. Based on ancient Indian records and inscriptions, the Kali yuga began 36 years after the Mahabharata War. Many scholars failed to calculate the accurate timing of Kurukshetra war, even if they did their methodology was wrong. It's quite understandable, 19th century Indologists didn't have the software tools like what we have now. I recalculated the accurate timing of both Kali Yuga and Mahabharata war using Astronomy simulation software, the details are given in Chapter-3. Where is Vedic Era Mount Meru located? No one really knows, where did Indo-Aryans come from?

Chapter-4 talks about the fascinating theory on **Cradle of Civilization**.

Archeological findings in the 17th century proved that several thousands of years before the arrival Aryans, a highly developed civilization existed to the south of the Godavari river (present day Telangana, Andhra Pradesh & Tamil Nadu). New details on the Veda Sila - a musical rock instrument precursor to Goddess Sarasvatī's Veena, totally ignored by the main stream media, which is situated on the banks of magnificent river Godavari. Chapter-5 provides an introduction to Vedic era goddess Sarasvatī, how a mythical river turned into a historical fact. It also talks about a brand new theory on the "Land of Seven Rivers".

Many people have a misconception that Lord Vishnu is a human manifestation of the supreme God who takes birth in each and every Yuga to uplift the Dharma. But, the true symbolism of Lord Vishnu is nothing but the Ananta or multiverse. Chapter-6 uncovers historical details of Lord Vishnu's reincarnations, popularly known as "Dashavatara", meaning ten avatars. Chapter-7 explores the brief history of Lord Shiva and also provides an introduction to Shaiva Agamas. Chapter-8 is about the history of a buffalo demon Mahishasura and the Goddess Mahishasura Mardini.

What is the true-life story of Buddha? What are the 'Four Famous Trees' and when did Buddha attain Mahaparinirvana? Chapter-9 has the details on historic Buddha. People hold some common perception on the year in which Jesus Christ was born, they think it's 0 CE, a beginning of the modern-day calendar. In fact, there is no such thing as 0 BCE or 0 CE, chapter-10 talks about Three-

Thousand-Year-Old Judea Prophecy and how an astronomy simulation software helps us to go back in time and uncover the true story of Jesus Christ, who undoubtedly a central figure of Christianity. When did Asura emperor Mahabali migrate to Pathalam or below Earth? In reality, it is below the equator, the history of Mahabali and the true symbolism of Vamana, discussed in Chapter-11. When did Ramayana happen? Chapter-12 talks about one of the most powerful Anti-Gods of Treta Yuga, daithya King Ravana. What is the true symbolism of Narakasura, the son of Earth, the details can be found in Chapter-13? Was Hitler a true Aryan? How an Austrian tramp could become the dictator of world's one of the most advanced nations of 20th Century? Chapter-14 talks about an Aryan dictator Adolf Hitler and his grand scheme of euthanasia and how it helped Nazis in implementing the "Final Solution" to eradicate the so called inferiors - Non-Aryans living in Germany.

According to Acharya Savitananda, the Supreme God is just one and only one and it is defined by austakshari mantra "BA-BA-NA-MA-KE-VA-LA-MA". No matter which faith or spiritual philosophy you follow, this book can certainly help you with the basic prerequisites required to attain infinite-consciousness through a simple 15-minute AM Bhakti Yoga and Meditation technique, as described in chapter-15.

Hatha Yoga is the basic form of Yoga and it's a prerequisite or preparation for an advanced Yoga method called "Raja Yoga" or Laya Yoga (Kundalini Yoga). If your goal is to get cure for alignments such as Chronic Fatigue, Insomnia, Stomach disorders, Chronic Headaches, Diabetes, Spine problems etc., how many pills do you want to swallow?

Practicing Raja Yoga is the solution, but you need to first start with basic form of Yoga and Meditation methods explained in chapter-16. An eight-hundred-year-old dance, Perini, the most vigorous and physically challenging dance of warriors; details about this ancient art can be found in Chapter-17.

Most of the terrorism related incidents occurring today can be linked to the religious hatred in one form or another. It's all happening because of the complete ignorance of the world history. Some of the religious fanatics think their God is better than another person's God. As a matter of fact, at the higher level of consciousness, the God is just one and only one, as revealed in the Agamas (Parmātma Darśana mandala 3, shloka 12) - **"paths are many but the Truth is one"**. Most of the books available on the shelves today preach you about the lost-faith, philosophy, and connection with God blah, blah, blah... But, there are some basic questions always unanswered. What is the true perception of God? Chapter-18 has the answer and scientific explanation to substantiate the theory is given elsewhere in the book.

Chapter-19 talks about the Vedic, Biblical & Puranic methods of Creationism and the true meaning of Avatars. Do you believe in re-incarnation? More than two billion people in the world think re-birth occurs based on Karma. Chapter-20 has details on the theory of re-incarnation. The purpose of this book is to encourage readers to seek Truth and attain Truth-Consciousness (also called as Universal-Consciousness or Infinite-Consciousness) and strive for longevity the way Gods and Anti-Gods did.

Gratitude is due to Archeological Survey of India (ASI), all the scholars whose work has been made use of, as acknowledged. Very special thanks are due to Shri Acharya Savitananda for teaching Bhakti Yoga and Meditation and allowing me to publish AM meditation techniques. Many thanks to my family and several friends for detailed suggestions for the improvement of the manuscript.

I take this opportunity to thank - Sirisha Reddy & Dr. Suman Reddy (Melbourne, Australia), L.V. Narasimha Reddy (Silicon Valley, California), Ravinder Reddy V (Virginia), M. Nitin Reddy (Fremont, California), Prasad Alluri (Intel Corporation, California), Thiruvengadam Manoharan (Folsom, California), Mallik Sajjanagandla (Broadridge Customer Communications, California),Veera Raju Vinnakota (Folsom, California), Prasad Pannala (AP, India), Ravi V Datla (Roseville, CA), Himanshu & Mukta Bharatiya (Folsom, California), Mathew Arcuri (Orlando Florida), Mark Loyer (Sacramento, California), Ramana Penumarty (Micron Corporation, California), Narendra Mikkilineni (Folsom, CA), and Suresh Madala (Folsom, CA) for the precious advice and critical insights on research, style and readability.

- L.H. Reddy (Folsom, California, 2018)

1. Introduction

That one Supreme reality has been styled
By various names by the learned seers,
They call one by many names.
They speak of Him as Indra, the Lord resplendent;
Mitra, the surveyor; Varuna, the virtuous;
Agni, the adorable;
Garutaman, the celestial and well-sung;
Yama, the ordainer; Matarishvan, the cosmic breadth.

(Rig Veda 1.164.46)

Is it History or Mythology?

Throughout the world history, one can find all sorts of movements such as anti-pollution, anti-immigration, anti-war, anti-nuclear or god delusion et cetera. But, is it possible to turn a movement on myth called "Lost Vedic Goddess Sarasvatī" into a historical fact? Is Ramayana real or a myth? What is the true symbolism of the demon Narakasura, the son of Earth? When did Asura King Bali migrate to Pathalam? What is the true meaning of Dashavatara? When did Mahabharata war occur? When did Kali Yuga begin and why the historians failed to find out the exact date?

One might wonder, why can't we simply turn to the history books in order to find out answers to these kind of trivial questions? Unfortunately, history books available in the academic circles today do not represent the true history of world's earliest Vedic Civilization. It's always flawed around unproven theory of AIT (Aryan Invasion Theory). According to AIT somewhere around 1500 BCE, Aryans invaded North India and destroyed the Indus Valley Civilization. But the text books still refer to such a false narrative, even though that theory had been debunked by the scientific community based on the lack of evidence. At the end of the last ice age, most of the ancient historical records were lost due to the series of deluges. These deluges occurred between the Sixteenth millennium BCE and the First millennium BCE. Fortunately, there are other types of tamper-proof sources available even today, this helps us to uncover the real history. One might question, what are these sources and why people didn't know about this until now?

The whole thing is a big political conspiracy, there are some special interest groups out there, who want to scale down the entire civilization to 4000 BCE as the starting point. Almost all the ancient history books were written based on this alternative fact of low chronology and they didn't give any credit to Ancient Indian Vedic Civilization that had been around for more than sixty thousand years. No one really knows how and when did the human race begin and where did we all come from. It might sound frivolous, but we should always be curious to find out what is the true story of human civilization on this planet Earth. A persistent question that always permeates our minds, is our civilization one-million-year-old or one-billion-year-old? Did humans migrate here from some other Galaxy or accidentally ended up here from some other Universe? Some paleontologists in India and California, even claimed that they found an evidence to support the theory that humans existed along with dinosaurs. There are a lot of unanswered questions about Darwin's theory of evolution. Is there any truth in the evolution theory based on natural selection or is it a colorful raconteur? Most of the theory of evolution is speculative in nature as the paleontologists didn't find any definitive information on the nature of the intermediate as well as about earliest organisms. Scientists found some variety of mosquitos or even crows didn't change a single bit in the last 40 million years, how is it possible and why the genetic mutation didn't occur if Darwin's theory of evolution is true. Several laboratory experiments by the scientists around the world failed to reproduce the kind of genetic mutation that proves the Darwin's theory.

The DNA evidence suggests that the continuity of human civilization has been happening in India for the last 84,000 years. There is also enough archeological evidence available today to prove that the cultural continuity happening in Central India for more than sixty thousand years. The evidence is based on the prehistoric (40,000BCE – 30,000BCE) paintings found in the Bhimbetka Rock Shelter Complex, Madhya Pradesh, India, which belongs to an anthropogenic culture (see illustration 1.6). The alternative sources such as astronomical references available in the ancient Vedic scriptures, Spaceborn RADAR Remote Sensing Images, DNA analysis, Philology, Ethnology, and Paleontology etc., collaborated the evidence found at various archeological sites. The epic story of Mahabharata has a reference to the Bhimbetka Rock Shelter. In the year 1954 CE, a geologist from Vikram University, V. S. Wakankar accidentally found Bhimbetka caves, which proved that the Pandavas rock shelter mentioned in the Mahabharata story is no longer a mythological fantasy but a real historical account. A similar type of evidence is found in several other places in India. So, it's time to revive the real ancient history based on these alternative sources of information.

It's absurd, Ancient Vedic Civilization didn't get any credit for their countless number of innovations in the fields of Vedic Astronomy, Medicine, Mathematics, Agriculture, Chemistry, Arts and Metallurgy. All these innovations took place several thousands of years before the beginning of industrial revolution. Rigveda and Samaveda mostly talk about the rituals and sacrifices as well as some description on Flying Vehicles, Astronomy, Geology and Geography etc., but the other two Vedas Atharva and Yajur refer to the mind boggling details about Brahmastra (an atomic weapon similar to or more powerful than modern atomic fission), electric and light powered machines etc. Ancient Indian Universities spread this Vedic knowledge to the entire world between 1000BCE and 1200 CE (see Appendix-II), which eventually paved a way to the discovery of modern technology.

Who were the Vedic Gods?

Rigveda, world's greatest and the oldest Vedic scripture tells us about ancient gods. The Vedic worshippers didn't have any means to measure the greatness of any particular god. They invoked the gods by chanting the hymns based on a particular occasion. The hymns confirm which god is too conspicuous whether Agni or Indra (Sun). Ancient gods were nothing but the personification of the supernatural powers such as Sun, Heavens, Galaxies and Constellations etc. Vedic gods of the highest order are Agni, the god of fire; Indra, the rain god or sometimes life giving Sun and the invisible deity Heavens or Dyaus. The priests invoke these gods by reading hymns at the regular intervals during a shiny beautiful day. If the day turns out to be terrible with dangerous thunderstorms and fearful lightning, the priests invoke the attendant gods (Anti-gods or Asuras) such as Aryaman or Mitra representing the same natural powers Sun and Heavens. Likewise, the other gods are Vishnu (personification of planet Mercury), Varuna - the god of wind, Soma - the lord of immortality, All-powerful enliven Sarasvatī - the goddess of music and Prithivi (Aditi) - the Goddess of Earth etc.

It might give us a false impression that the Vedic civilization supported polytheism? But, in reality it's just one and only one God as mentioned in the RV (Rig Veda - 1.164.46); a translated version of hymn given at the beginning of this chapter. The Rig-Vedic sages worshipped just the symbols and did not build any temples or idols. The concept of metaphysical connection with God or idol worship developed at the later stage during Puranic period (4000 BCE – 1000 BCE).

The central theme of the Vedic Knowledge was Astronomy with numerous references to the Nakshatras (Constellations). In Vedas, the heavenly bodies or Nakshatras oftentimes referred to as Devatas (Gods). The Rig-Vedic priests indirectly offered prayers to Heaven or Earth by invoking the fire god, Agni. Many 19th century western translators of RV misrepresented Daksha as the shady god and father of Mitra and Varuna. But, Mr. Bala Gangadhar Tilak resolved the perplexity around this Daksha by identifying it with Orion constellation. Similarly, Goddess Aditi was sometimes identified with

Sky and some other times as Earth and Heaven. The process of personification or the measure of personality with an object of worship took several thousand years and it never completely attained to the minds of ancient Vedic people, not until the Puranic Period. The deity Sun was the only one evolved as the powerful object of worship and later on goddess Gayatri and Goddess Sarasvatī gained attention.

The Vedic Rishis blamed the South as the Asuras (anti-gods or Demons). The Vedas refer to Rakshasas, Sambara, Vritras, Panis, Atris, Vala and Namuchi as Asuras. Not sure, who these people are? Some hymns refer to the native people or Dravidian rulers and some other hymns refer to the Stars of Southern Hemispheric night sky? The Vedas in the present form written from ancient Sanskrit scriptures sometime around 1300 BCE. Before that it was in an oral form for several thousands of years (since 24,000 BCE). The bulk of the Vedic material is taken from the Dravidian traditions, and some material also taken from the original Aryan Milieu. Rigveda contains 1017 hymns and its divided into Ten mandalas (books). Out of 10 mandalas, seven Mandalas belong to Deccan and South Indian seers which they inherited it from their ancestors. The Vedic Samhitās are the ancient Sanskrit family collections of various Sages which were passed on from one generation to another in the oral form.

Timeline of Vedic Astronomy

Lord Vishnu, a personification of planet mercury, was a minor Vedic deity in the beginning. But, later on became the God of Ananta (multiverse) during the Puranic period. As per legends, Lord Vishnu was the first Dravidian to introduce Astronomy to the ancient world. This can be validated based on numerous references available in Puranas and Mahabharata about the pole star Vega (Abhijit) falling below the horizon. The Astronomical simulation of heavens[1] (see illustrations 1.1 & 1.2) showed that the star Vega fell below the horizon around 23, 998 BCE, hence this must be the time of Lord Vishnu during which he existed. The reincarnation of Lord Vishnu occurred in the form of Avatars. This process of re-incarnation is a hypothetical situation, where Sages assign the people with super human skills as an incarnate of Lord Vishnu. So far, the Sages assigned nine avatars and the tenth one yet to come.

Vedic Samhitas

Vedic Sages played a vital role of cardinal significance in shaping the ancient civilizations. They were the pioneers of spirituality, who inspired the ancient world through their intellectual property called Nigama and Agama Shāstras. Nigamas and Agamas are also known as Śruti, meaning in Sanskrit "what has been revealed by the God and heard by Sages who compiled it". Nigamas are the ancient Vedic Samhitas which are non-religious revelations, compiled on the banks of Godavari, Sarasvatī and her seven sister rivers (popularly known as Sapta Sindhavah) between 24,000 BCE and 4,000 BCE. Based on the geological and remote-sensing data, the river Sarasvatī lost its perennial status sometime after 5500 BCE and it totally dried up around 1900 BCE. It's almost impossible to find out the exact dateline of Rig-Veda, but Vedas refer to Sarasvatī as the mighty river, which confirms that the Vedas were probably compiled before 5,500 BCE. Vedic Sages were the global ambassadors with a special privilege to longevity. Based on Puranic scriptures, the average life expectancy during Vedic period was more than 175 years. What is the secret behind their longevity?

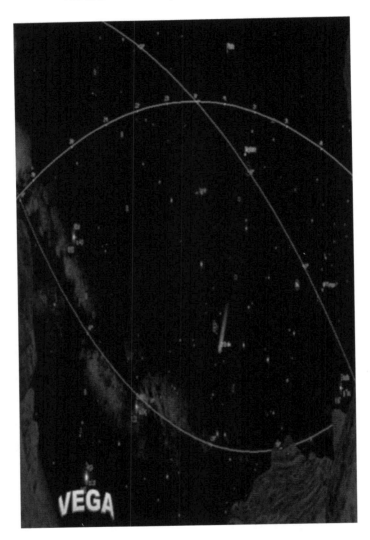

Illustration 1.1: A Simulated View of Heavens in the year 23,998 BCE which confirms that the Pole star Vega fell below the horizon during that time. Vedic Scriptures and Mahabharata constantly talk about pole star Vega "Abhijit falling down" which confirms that Lord Vishnu, the first Vedic astronomer, probably lived during that time.

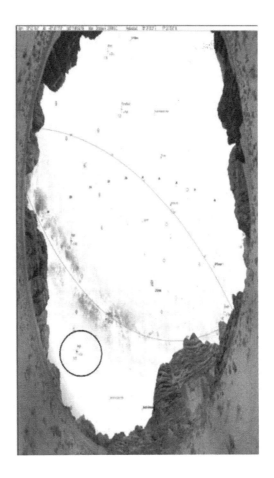

Illustration 1.2: Another simulated view where the current pole star Vega (within circle) almost falling below horizon in the year 23998 BCE. This Vega 'falling down' mentioned in the Puranic texts confirms that the Vedic sages were probably observing the heavens since such time.

It could be attributed to some of the factors such as Soma (a Divinely Drink extracted from Soma Plant), Panchamrita (Cow Milk; Curd Rice or Barley Khichdi cooked with dhaniya, haldee and lentils; Honey; Ghee and Fruits), Apsarasas (Companionship of Dice playing and Dancing

Heavenly Nymphs), and Yoga & Meditation (an ancient Spiritual Science of Hindus). They influenced the Earthlings from their global headquarters located on the top of mount Meru. Where is mount Meru situated? A question that was never answered to anybody's satisfaction till date.

Puranic Gods

Apart from the Vedas, Agamas are the highest spiritual authority on Sānatana Dharma. Āgamas are Non-Vedic spiritual scriptures derived from Shiva Siddhanta, compiled by the Dravidian and Himalayan Shiddas around 4000 BCE or later. Some people call Agama Siddhanta as the 5th Veda. Based on the descriptions found in Agamas, the Dravidians contributed to the development of Architecture, Agriculture, Medicine, Fine Arts, Metallurgy and Chemical Engineering. Lord Shiva was centered as the main deity in Agamas, replacing Vedic god Rudra as the prominent deity during the Puranic era. As per the Jaiminigrhyasūtra, Lord Shiva becomes the main deity, the life-giving Sun in the Post-Vedic era. The table 1.1 shows the classification of various heavenly objects representing Vedic, Puranic, Greek and Roman gods and their primary roles.

Vedic gods were in existence till 5,500 BCE, after that the Puranic gods took precedence, around 2000 BCE all other gods such as Roman, Greek, Hebrew, Egyptian etc. were in existence. After Shaka era (78 CE), instead of the main gods, their incarnations gained importance. The Vedic deity Soma or Moon becomes Umā (Lord Shiva's wife) in the Puranas, Jupiter becomes Brahma, Venus becomes Indra and Saturn represents Yama (Table 1.1). Similarly, Lord Shiva's son Skanda becomes the planet Mars, in Southern India Skanda is also known as Karthikeya or Murugan or Subramanyam. Other deities were re-assigned in the Puranas based on their importance.

Heavenly object	Vedic God	Puranic God	Greek / Roman God	Description
Sun	Indra	Shiva	Zeus	Ruler of the Gods
Moon	Soma	Umā		Goddess Shakti, Shiva's wife in Puranas. God of immortality in Veda.
Mercury	Vishnu	Vishnu	Hermes	Creator of multiverse, supreme God Vishnu in Puranas, minor deity in Veda, Messenger of the Gods in Greek
Saturn	Yama	Yama	Cronus	Dual God in Veda & Puranas; the God of Sky in Greek; Ruler of Titans in Roman
Venus	Vena	Indra	Aphrodite	Indra demoted in puranic time
Jupiter	Brihas pati	Brahma	Zeus	The Sage of the Gods in Veda; Creator in Puranas; the ruler of the Gods in Roman & Greek

Table 1.1: Comparison of Vedic vs Puranic gods

How did Vedic Gods transform the ancient world?

During the ancient times, crossing the Vindhyas was not possible. An impenetrable thick rain forest called "Mahākāntāra" isolated the Deccan from Northern India. It's much easier to cross Van Allen radiation belt and land on the Moon than crossing the Vindhyas from Deccan to enter Northern India or vice versa. Padma Sri L.S. Wakankar tells us Lord Shiva and his followers migrated from South[2]. They went through the ancient Isthmus at the Vindhyan arm of North-central hilly route. After crossing Vindhyas continued towards north and established in the Mount Kailas. After which, the North India started getting more pilgrims and more importance.

In reality, the twelve Jyothilingas of Lord Shiva represent the true geography of the sacred Bharata and the common people didn't need any maps to explore ancient India its already built into their minds. The main contributions of Lord Shiva to the humanity was Yoga, Meditation and Shiva Thandavam, a type of dance. Performing Shiva Thandavam and Meditation helps human beings in attaining pure-consciousness, improved self-esteem, vitality and longevity. The main contributions of Lord Vishnu to the humanity was Vedic Astronomy. The Dravidian Siddhas contributed to the development of Ayurveda and Vastu.

The Vedic Astrology or Jyothisya, consisting of three branches, which are 1) Khagola Sastra - Vedic Astronomy or study of heavens 2) Ayurveda – a medical branch and 3) Vastu - an architectural branch. Vedic Astrology played an integral role in socio-economic development of the ancient societies. In the absence of GPS or Compass during the ancient times, Vedic astronomy was the only solution to find out the sea routes, just like how penguins find their way back home. Ayurveda is still a solution to many diseases which modern medicine failed to cure. Ancient architectural knowledge - Vastu is in usage even today, people follow this for the house and temple constructions. Vedic Calendar was instrumental in determining the arrival of monsoons, beginning of agriculture season, choosing muhurtham for marriages and tithi for festival celebrations etc. Both heavenly gods and the human manifestations of heavenly objects contributed to the advancement of human civilization.

Who were the Aryans?

The original meaning of the word Aryan was "People of Plough Cultivation". And it seems to have underwent semantic changes over the time as shown in the table 1.2. The scholars, in general, agree that the word "Aryan" doesn't denote any human race. But a form of address representing the people's occupation or profession.

Meaning of the word Aryan	Period	Name of the Era
Plough Cultivator	15000 BCE - 5000 BCE	Pre-Vedic
Noble Person	5000 BCE - 4000 BCE	Indo-European Era
One who observes the rules of the social system.	4000 BCE - 500 BCE	Late-Vedic
Ideal Man	500 BCE onwards	Hindu, Jainism & Buddhism Era

Table 1.2: Classification of Aryan through ages

The 19th Century European Indologists predicted a theory that the Aryans were the Indo-Europeans. the original horse riding people of Euro-Russia and who invaded India around 1500 BCE. Yet, the DNA evidence proved otherwise, the parental haplogroup R1a1 originated in India. Hence, the Aryans were of Indian origin and Aryan invasion theory (AIT) is not valid anymore[3]. Based on the latest DNA evidence, Africa is not the cradle of civilization, the out of Africa theory proved to be wrong[3]. The DNA analysis also confirmed that the maternal lineages of the rest of the world is originated from India. Whatever may be the origin of Aryans but they played a central role in safe guarding Vedas in oral form from generation to generation.

Vedic Myths

Vedic civilization worshiped the light and other supernatural powers, they had an aspiration to immortality and self-discipline to the Truth. Swami Dayananda was a great Sanskrit scholar and founder of Arya Samaj. He made a remarkable attempt to establish Veda as a living religious scripture. Mr. T. P. Aiyer has attempted to prove that the Rik is the Symbolic representation of the Earth's geo-phenomenon. Mr. Tilak argued that the Vedic home located at Arctic circle[4]. Sri Aurobindo made a bold attempt to prove that Vedas played a double role; primary role which is a psychological function of spiritual enlightenment and self-culture and in the secondary role served as the media of worship for the Rishis.

But these are all myths, there is no evidence available to substantiate the claims, an exchange of falsehood for the sacrifice of Truth. The Vedic scriptures not associated with any religion. The hotri (Vedic reciters of Rig-Veda) invoke the gods (natural powers) by reading the hymns aloud. So, the Rik (Rig Veda) is not a symbolism for Earth's Geo-Phenomenon. There is no archeological evidence found to prove Mr. Tilak's claim of Arctic home. Sri Aurobindo may be correct up to some extent, but I still have an issue with his deviation from the commentary of Sayana (15th Century Deccan poet who provided commentary on Vedas, without which it would have been impossible to fully understand the ancient Sanskrit meaning). Let us look at the following passage, I am particularly interested in the interpretation of the last stanza.

"Kavī no mitrāvarunā,
tuvijātā uruksayā;
dakṣaṁ dadhāte apasam."

According to Sri Aurobindo:

"Finally, we have the goddess Dakshina who may well be a female form of Daksha, himself a god and afterwards in the Purana one of the Prajapatis, the original progenitors, —we have Dakshina associated with the manifestation of knowledge and sometimes almost identified with Usha, the divine Dawn, who is the bringer of illumination. I shall suggest that Dakshina like the more famous Ila, Sarasvatī and Sarama, is one of four goddesses representing the four faculties of the Ritam or Truth- consciousness..."

The Dakshina is not a female form of Daksha as interpreted by Sri Aurobindo. It's a sacrifice given to observe an astronomical event related to Daakshayani the daughter of Daksha Prajapathi (Orion constellation), it typically includes anything from land, cows, rice (one Chatta or one bag) to Soma-wine. The Vedic ritual sites no longer exist in India, but some people in Deccan still follow the Vedic traditions even today.

Antiquity of Vedas and Agamas

Astronomical references found in Mahabharata proves that the approximate timeline of Gayatri Mantra as 7500 BCE. Even though Vedic hymns might have been recited as early as 7500 BCE, the actual commencement of Vedic literature started at much later period. Vedic sages compiled Vedas in an oral tradition to teach their Shisyas (pupils) by recitation. For an average student, it took almost twelve years to recite, memorize and understand one Samhita. And more than 40 years to master all the four Vedic Samhitas – Rig, Sama, Yajur, and Atharva. Don't freak out!!! The life expectancy during Vedic times was 175 years. The legendary Kshatriya King turned Sage, Vishvamitra compiled the first hymn of Rig Veda, popularly known as Gayatri Mantra, on the banks of Godavari, later the mythical river Sarasvatī became the cradle of High Vedic Civilization[5]. The river Godavari, Ganges of Deccan born in the western Ghats and flows into Telangana before emptying through seven mouths into the Bay of Bengal. The Rigveda called the people of Deccan (Indian states of Telangana and parts of Maharashtra) as Turvashas.

According to Prof. Max Muller, Vedic literature can be divided into four periods, namely Chhandas, Mantra, Brâhmana and Sutra period. Dr. Haug, by assigning 500 years for each period based on comparison with Chinese literature arrives at 2400 BCE – 2000 BCE as the starting period of Vedic literature. It's hard to find out the true antiquity of Agamas (Shaiva Siddhanta). Based on the archeological evidence the Siddhas might have compiled the initial versions of Agamas around 4000 BCE[12]. The river culture of Vedic poetry might have started from the deep south. The recent developments pushed the antiquity of Rig-Veda to the 10,000 BCE and beyond[11]. Professor Max Müller proposed the lower chronology theory, which argues that the date of compilation of Rigveda as 1200 BCE. Max Müller who was a German born 19th century Indologist undermined Vedas in the name of linguistic method of ascertaining the age. Many believed Max Müller proposed his theory to please his colonial missionary bosses. In fact, an advanced civilization did exit in India, several thousands of years before the arrival of western merchants, who later colonized India. As per Moriz Winternitz, a nineteenth century European researcher, the pre-Christian European civilization was younger than the Vedic culture. But, no one contradicted Max Muller's lower chronology[7], until an Indian Politician cum lawyer B. G. Tilak noticed this in the early 1890's.

The great Indian scholar Bal Gangadhar Tilak, contradicted Max Muller's theory in 1893 CE. Based on the astronomical methods, Tilak proposed a new high antiquity of the Vedas to more than 6000 BCE. Several years later, Max Muller retracted his statement about lower chronology. He admitted that his theory was a mere empirical work in his book "The Six systems of Indian Philosophy". The year 6676 BCE or 6677 BCE, was the beginning of Vedas according to the Greek historians Pliny and Arrian. They based their analysis on the historical recordings of Megasthenes, a Greek Ambassador to the courts of the Emperor Chandragupta, in the year 300 BCE[11].

Based on the astronomical references, Sage Vishwamitra compiled the Rigveda sometime around 7500 BCE. Mahabharata mentions (Aadiparva A.71 & Ashwamedha A.44), Sage Vishwamitra initiated the new time reference. He broke the tradition and counted the first Nakshatra at the Autumnal Equinox. The older traditions before Vishwamitra time started counting at Vernal Equinox. Dr. P.V. Vartak tells us star Shraavana was at the Vernal equinox, around 7500 BCE. So, this must be the period of Ramayana during which Sage Vishwamitra existed[9].

Origin of Sanskrit Language

In ancient India, the Kshatriyas, Merchants and Daivajnas of Deccan needed a new language. A language intelligible to all the people of North, South and North east India. Thus, the Sanskrit language was the natural solution. Panini, architected the Sanskrit grammar in the 6th Century BCE. He adopted the grammatical rules from dravidian languages, but mostly from Telugu language related to 'sandhi' and 'samāsamulu'. In the ancient times, Telugu was known as either Tenuṅgu or Teliṅga or Telingana. Based on the archeological evidence, the Sanskrit language in the present form was compiled sometime around 1200 BCE. There is a version of Telugu spoken in Andhra and Karnataka border districts modelled around 1300 CE based on Sanskrit language, but the Telugu has Ten dialects (including Gondi, a language spoken by tribal people in Gondwana region of Telangana) and some of them are much older (> 4000 BCE) than any other Dravidian language.

The 3rd Century BCE inscriptions of the Emperor Ashoka has the Telugu words. An inscription found in Gujarat (Sankheda, 594 CE) which uncovered usage of decimal system for the first time to the world has Telugu words. Telugu seers developed the language script somewhere around 6th century BCE. Before that either Brahmi or Prakriti script was used to write Telugu. Until 17th century CE, Celtic or any other Indo-European language didn't have any type of grammar. But, in 1861 CE, Max Mūller and his German colleagues adopted it from the Dravidian languages and popularized it in the Europe. This proves that Sanskrit didn't have any grammar to begin with but it later on adopted it from Telugu and other Dravidian languages.

The Dravidians were the first people to come up with the grammar. It is like an Error Correction Code used in the digital transmissions. Once a scripture or poem compiled with proper grammar it's almost impossible to alter it. This kind of grammatical protection was needed to transmit the literature in the oral form. The whole Southern India was affected by series of deluges since 16,000 BCE, it was impossible to preserve the manuscripts other than in the oral form. Based on the etymological method, it's possible to prove that Telugu is much older than any other Dravidian language. The following is the information about the antiquity of Telugu language found in Encarta and Encyclopedia of Britannica:

"Telugu is the only Dravidian language that has the features such as the Vowel harmony in suffix. The nouns found in Telugu has some unusual features. Such as masculine or feminine in the singular, and rational or non-rational in the plural. The pronouns in Telugu are so complex, it's not only based on the gender system but also based on the social status. This type of pronouns not found in any other Dravidian or Ancient Sanskrit language, which proves that all other Indian languages have not fully evolved and not as ancient as Telugu language."

Soma Wine – A Divine Drink

Rituals and sacrifices were the integral part of the Vedic traditions; 9ᵗʰ Mandala of Rik has the details on Soma sacrifice. In Vedas, Soma-wine was once considered the drink of Gods, the Vedic symbol of bliss and Ananda, and now it's the drink of the Tribal. Soma-wine would be part of the Dakshina given to the priest, Ayavarulu or Adhvaryu – an Atharva-Vedic reciter. The village rock fort once used to be the home to many Vedic Sages was built during the ancient times (see illustration 1.3). The village is situated within 100 Km radius of Godavari river and Dharmapuri town which was once center for one of the largest settlements of Vedic Pundits. The Soma wine extracted from the flowers of Vippa Tree (binomial name - Madhuca Longifolia), and it has no symbolism other than the pure drink of intoxication or Vippa Saara. It is a tropical tree found in Telangana, South India and various parts of central India. The flowers resemble Moon shape, hence the name Soma (see illustration 1.4).

Illustration 1.3: Thorlikonda Rock Fort cum Shelter Entrance (built during the ancient times). Till late 1980s, it used to have a great bath and Vedic ritual place inside the fort and now its replaced with other modern temple structures. The history is lost forever, but, the two horse heads (carved out of monolithic rock) present on the fort entrance and author's childhood memories are still the first-hand witnesses of the existence of Vedic Culture in rural India.

I think pretty much all the scholars got it wrong about Soma. They all mentioned its either psychological function or creative function of the Moon. But the Soma-wine has nothing to do with any imaginary function, other than a pure intoxication liquid. Till late 1980s, in my native village Thorlikonda (Nizamabad Dist., Telangana, India), where

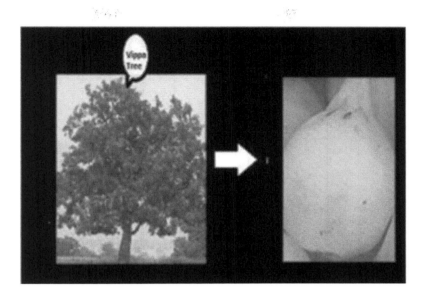

Illustration 1.4: Vippa flowers from which Soma-wine extracted.

The juice extracted from Vippa flowers tastes good in the morning. The fermentation process happens with the help of the deities Indra (Sun light) and Vayu (air). It should only be consumed till certain time around noon or early afternoon; after that it turns out sour and even the birds won't like it, therefore it should be thrown out. The concept of Divya Gaudiya or auspicious occasion was probably derived from this concept of Soma fermentation process.

Chronology

(from Precambrian to 100 CE)

Commonly used Abbreviations:
BCE - Before Common Era
BC - Before Christ
CE- Common Era
AD - Anno Domini

Period	Historical event
4,500,000,000 BCE	Speculated age of Earth by the modern scientists.
4,320,000,000 BCE	Speculated cosmic age of the Universe as mentioned in the Vedas (Rigveda - IV.58.3) more than 7000 years ago.
3,000 Million BCE	Based on Precambrian fossils (3 to 4 billion years ago), Cyanobacteria, a single cell organism (blue-green algae) played a vital role in formation of Oxygenated Atmosphere, which led to the beginning life on the planet Earth. How did this single cell begin? Scientists are still trying to find out about this. According to the Puranas, the Lord Brahma creates the life on the earth. The Ananta (Infinite) god Vishnu creates the Lord Brahma. Lord Brahma is the symbolism for Galaxies, Earth and the Universe whereas Lord Vishnu is the symbolism for Multiverse. The comets or meteors transport the life-forming bacteria within the Galaxy.
650 Million BCE to 600 Million BCE	Geological formation of Peninsular India consisting of ancient crystalline rocks, the oldest of the three units India made of. The other two younger units are: The Himalayan Mountain

	system and Indo-Gangetic alluvial plains.
300 Million BCE to 200 Million BCE	Towards end of Paleozoic Era, all the land masses coalesced to form a super continent called Pangaea. The ancient ocean Tethys separated southern continent Gondwana (South India, South America, Australia, South Africa) from the northern continent Laurasia (North America, Europe. Russia, China)
6,60,000 BCE	Speculative beginning of human race and beginning of Yuga Cycle as mentioned in Vayu Purana (70.48). Based on Puranas, each Yuga cycle known as Kalpa is made of 12,000 years[15]. That is the day of Brahma consisting of four Yugas. The Kurta yuga lasts for 4000 years, the Treta yuga for 3000 years, Dwapara for 2000 years, Kali yuga for 1000 years and an additional 2000 years for the transition period (Sandhya) between each Yuga. At the end of 12,000-year cycle of Kalpa, the civilization would be completely lost due to any number reasons such as deluges, wars, asteroid impacts, ice age etc. Within the next 1000 years, the sages who ever survived in the mountain caves would help re-write Vedas and rebuild the civilization which paves a way to the beginning of another Yuga cycle. Present day, we are in the 55th yuga cycle. During the 1st Century CE, the length of each Kalpa was increased to ridiculously longer period of 306,720,000 years from the original period of 12,000 years with an

	intention to measure the age of cosmos.
1,60,000 BCE	Speculative immigration of 'Homo Sapiens Sapiens' out of Africa theory by Cann and Stoneking, Stinger (1987); Andews (1988) and Recombinant DNA study sponsored by IBM (2011). The DNA Male Groups A & B and female sub-groups L0-L6 proves otherwise; the African Specific Lineages never went out of Africa. Some other researchers suggest they probably went outside East Africa towards south east Asia and Australia at least once, but never survived after the first ice age. All the European, Asian, Australia and Amerindian maternal lineages originated from India (source Metspalu et al, 2004).
83,000 BCE	Journey of a first man out of India towards Australia. (Based on DNA analysis by B.P. Hudjasove, 2007)
72,000 BCE – 63,000 BCE	Worst Glacial Phase, world population completely whipped out in the northern Hemisphere, except in India, Africa and east Asia.
50000 BCE to 40000 BCE	Beginning of rural agriculture in South and Central India.
40000 BCE to 30000 BCE	Domestication of horses in India; Bhimbetka Cave paintings shows that the horse riding culture existed in India for more than 50 thousand years (see figure 1.8).

37,000 BCE to 11,000 BCE	Adamgrah rock paintings located on the south of Narmada river at Adamgrah Hills, Madhya Pradesh, India. Popular for existence of pre-historic art culture, the rock paintings found in red and white colors.
35000 BCE to 30000 BCE	Domestication of Oxen and beginning of Millet cultivation on the banks of Godavari river in Deccan and South India. Discovery of Wheel and Bullock cart by the Dravidians.
30,000 BCE to 25,000 BCE	Beginning of Agriculture in Deccan – Sugar cane, Maize, Cotton, Silk, Turmeric, and Jowar. Bāsanghi Rice Cultivation in Telangana, a rice crop that grows for six months as against 4-month crops available today. Similarly, beginning of 18-month old sugar cane crop cultivation; present day crop is 9-month old. (Based on the Paleobotany findings by the agriculture researchers in Hyderabad, India)
24000 BCE to 19500 BCE	Speculative period during which the Dravidian Astronomer, Lord Vishnu invented Vedic Astronomy, who was the minor deity during Vedic Period and later became the Supreme Deity during the Puranic Times. (Based on the astronomical references found in Mahabharata and Puranas)
19,000 BCE to 17000 BCE	First Ancient Tamil Sangam Period[13]. Development of ancient Sanskrit, Telingana (ancient Telugu) and Dravida (Ancient Tamil) languages. Ancient Tamil and ancient Sanskrit no longer exist today, whereas ancient Telugu is still spoken in some parts of Telangana State.

14,058 BCE	First deluge submerging parts of Kumari Kandam into the Indian Ocean[10].
14,000 BCE to 9,500 BCE	Speculative dateline of Aryan immigration into India through the river mouths of Godavari, Cauvery, Ganga, Thunghabadra, Narmada and Sarasvatī (via sea routes). Aryans initially took up Agriculture jobs and later on introduced to the Vedic studies and rituals by the Dravidian ruling clan Kshatriyas.
11,000 BCE to 8,000 BCE	Proto-Astronomy instrument to record Moon phases belongs to upper Paleolithic period, Lunar Calendar Stick, found in Nicobar Islands, India (see illustration 1.5).
9564 BCE	According to Tamil records, Cataclysm aftermath of ice age submerged the ancient Dravidian cities into Bay of Bengal and separated Lanka from main land India. The massive amount of geological changes to Vindhyas mountain range, completely isolated Deccan from the rest of North India. Submerged large parts of Kumari Kandam (a south Indian Ocean Island which was a speculated common home for Indo-Europeans, Indo-Iranians and Indo-Aryans, a theory proposed by author in chapter-4).
7500 BCE to	Gayatri Mantra, first set of Vedic hymns, compilation by Kshatriya King turned Sage Vishvamitra on the Banks of Godavari.; the dateline was based on the Astronomical reference of Sravana being the first Nakshatra at

7400 BCE	Autumnal Equinox found in Mahabharata and Puranas, Sage Vishvamitra introduced this new time reference. At the same time, compilation of Rig-Veda in oral form, a combined effort by the Himalayan Sages and the Dravidian Siddhas on the Banks of Lost Vedic river Sarasvatī.
7300 BCE to 7200 BCE	Age of Ramayana; existence of bio-chemical based flying machines in Deccan and Lanka.
7100 BCE to 6500 BCE	Beginning of migration of Dravidians from South India towards North-west to escape from deluges. Archeological Society of India (ASI) excavations at Bhirana and Dholavira (present day Gujarat, India) proved that they represented a type of highly advanced urban civilization, now known as Harappan civilization. As per legend an unknown Dravidian King invaded Egypt in a horse chariot and established the dynasty that lasted for more than 4 centuries. During this time the Egyptians learned brick construction, lift irrigation methods and agriculture techniques from Dravidians. As a result of this stone age culture in Egypt suddenly transformed into a highly sophisticated civilization.
6676 BCE	As per the records of Greek historians Pliny and Arrian, beginning of ancient Hindu Calendar system based on Saptarishi used in some parts of North India and Tribal people of Deccan. It's an Ancient Indian calendar system based on the stars of Ursa Major.

6,500 BCE to 5000 BCE	Beginning of wheat cultivation in North India and Saraswati-Indus valley. The DNA, Super family language immigration and archeological evidence shows that the Indo-European, Indo-Iranian and Indo-Aryan migration out of India towards Anatolia, middle east, Central Asia and Europe. Based on the research conducted by Malti Shndge of Pune, Maharashtra, India; Sumerian and Akkadian languages of Mesopotamia are the offshoots of Sanskrit language because of its close affinity. Based on the paper published by Prof. K.D. Abhyankar, Indian National Science Academy (INSA), Hyderabad, Telangana, India, the Parsis of Arianavayo (presumed an earlier home of Aryans) talk about the mystic river goddess Saraswati and whereas Vedas don't talk about Aryans, which proves that Indo-Aryans migrated out of India. Speculative beginning of Mesopotamia civilization started by Indo-Europeans who moved out of India.
5000 BCE	Vedic Sarasvatī river lost its perennial status presumably due to the plate tectonic activity, the evidence is based on Satellite images taken by ISRO (Indian Research Space Organization). As shown in figure 5.8, the RADARSAT paleo-channel

	(PC) image delineated rivers Yamuna and Sutlej watershed as the major contributors to the mighty waters of Vedic Saraswati. After major earthquake, the present day river Sutlej moved westwards and separated from Sarasvatī'. At the same time another major perennial source drifted away eastwards and merged into the present-day river Yamuna.
4,600 BCE	Speculated date of Taittiriya Brahmana (TB) composed in present form, one of the earliest Rig-Vedic (Samhitā) text describing Vedic science. It also mentioned about the Ramayana author Valmiki.
4,200 BCE	Beginning of copper metallurgy in Indo-Gangatic plains.
3700 BCE	Battle of Ten Kings mentioned in Vedas, the evidence was based on radio-carbon testing of bronze statue head of Sage Vasistha[8] found near Delhi (Carbon-14 test range of 4500 BCE to 3700 BCE). The history is lost in the archeological context because it was transported out of India. The bronze head is now in possession of Hicks foundation, California.
3600 BCE	Completion of Vedic Canon (Rik, Yajur, Sama and Atharva Veda)
3,500 BCE	Beginning of Maha-Shivaratri in Deccan and other places [Kaushitaki

to 3,000 BCE	Brahmana 19.3]. Beginning of the new year based on Amanta scheme as interpreted by the scholars Oldenburg and Weber [1914], Caland [1931], Abhyankar [1998].
3,138 BCE	Timeline of Mahabharata war – the last time when Gods, Rakshasas and Men roamed together the Planet Earth.
3,102 BCE	End of Dwapara yuga and beginning of new era, known as **Kali Yuga**. ‡‡ Based on Puranas, each Kalpa is made of 12,000 years. That is the day of Brahma consisting of four Yugas. The Kurta yuga lasts for 4800 years, the Treta yuga for 3600 years, Dwapara for 2400 years and Kali yuga for 1200 years. This includes the twilight zone or Sandhya between each yuga. Its 800 years between Kruta yuga and Treta yuga; 600 years between Treta and Dwapara and 400 years between Dwapara and Kali. The Yuga concept was developed based on the previous deluges. According to which, the whole civilization ends at the end of 12000-year yuga cycle. The Sages predicted people in Kaliyuga live with diminished moral values and less intellectual capabilities as compared to the previous Yuga. Fortunately, the world didn't end after the great floods in 1900 BCE and 1750BCE. We are thus, still in this dark age of Kaliyuga with presumably diminished moral values and less intellectual capabilities.

	Around 1st century CE, the Kaliyuga was extended to abnormally longer period of 432,000 years. ‡‡ The 5-year or 6-year Yuga concept used for Adhikamāsa (synchronization of Lunar and Solar Calendars) is different from the Kali Yuga. The Kalpa consisting of four yugas (Kruta, Treta, Dwapara and Kali) was used for estimating the age of the Universe (i.e. age of Lord Brahma) during the puranic era.
3001 BCE	Compilation of Sulva Sutras, a Vedic Mathematics which explains Decimal numbers, number zero, infinite, area of Triangle, Linear algebra and quadratic equations and various theorems (including a theorem similar to Pythagoras). Vedic mathematics was used to calculate the star positions. Ancient Indians were the first people to discover zero, decimal, infinite and Pythagoras theorem.
3000 BCE	Satapatha Brahmana (SB) composed, ancient Vedic Indian science explaining Geometry, Mathematics and the names of 27 Naksatras [Seidenberg 1962, 1978, 1983]. SB also provides details about the Agnichayana alter construction made of bricks. Agnichayana rite which symbolizes Cosmos is a Twelve-day ritual that takes place in the Mahavedi (a large Trapezoidal area made of bricks) before beginning the yearlong ritual in order to synchronize the lunar and solar year. Based on the astronomical interpretations of SB 2.1.2.3 by Weber [1861], Dikshit [1895], Achar [2000], Subhash Kak [2011] and Prasanna [2011], the Krittikas

	[Pleiades] were always seen due east, near equator or the declination was almost zero, this leads to the dateline of 3000BCE.
2200 BCE	Decline of Harappan civilization due to persisting large scale drought in the Gaggar-Hakra (Vedic Saraswati) basin (Figure 1.7)
1900 BCE to 1700 BCE	Vedic Saraswati river completely dried up.
1000 BCE - 600 CE	Several Ancient Universities (Nagarjuna, Nalanda, Takshasilā, etc.) established in Indian sub-continent with more than 10000 students from Middle East (Arabs), China, Europe and Asia (see Appendix-II).
500 BCE	Beginning of Satavahana Dynasty (Telingana or Telugu speaking people) in Deccan and later expanded to North and South India.
100 CE -300 CE	Hindu Philosophical thought - the Dharma Shāstras (Manu Dharma-Shastra, Kama sutra, Artha-shastra) were composed
100 CE – 900 CE	Bhakti movement in India. Revival of Vaishnavism and Shaivism. Jainism lost its appetite and Buddhism virtually kicked out of India.
476 CE – 550 CE	Aryabhata, famous Vedic astronomer and Mathematician from Pataliputra (Patna, India) who could solve quadratic equations, provided the scientific explanation of Solar and Lunar eclipses first time to the world, at the age of 23. There are some minor errors in his geometric formulas but he created long lasting influence on Arabic science with his work 'Āryabhatīya'; Arabs called him Arjehir.
	Brahmugupta wrote a text 'Brahma-sphuta-siddhanta' explaining Indian astronomy including solar and lunar eclipses, Siddhantas, algebraic equations,

598CE - 670CE	celestial sphere and instruments to compute planet and star positions. That's how Arabs and rest of the world learned about Mathematics and Astronomy. Muhammad al-Fazari translated Brahmugupta's work into Arabic with the help of Ujjain scholar Kankah in the year 770 CE

Illustration 1.5: Proto-Astronomy instrument to record Moon phases belongs to upper Paleolithic period, Lunar Calendar Stick, found in Nicobar Islands (India), dated between 11,000 BCE and 8,000 BCE. This shows that the Tribals in Indian sub-continent involved in Astronomy for more than ten thousand years.

Illustration 1.6: Proof of early Vedic Astronomy – Indus valley civilization used birth seals written in Harappan script (around 3500 BCE) most likely depicts the birth time based on the positions of stars and Nakshatras (constellations) used by the proto-Dravidians. Many historians interpreted it differently, Harappan script is not yet deciphered, so it's anybody's guess, no one knows the exact meaning for sure. But, there were no three animals lived in the past, so these seals most likely represent the Janmapatrika, a birth certificate written based on birth stars, animals representing constellations and the Gotra. This kind of practice is still followed in the rural India except the fact that the zodiac symbols changed over the period of 5,000 years. (Photo credit: Archeological Survey of India).

Illustration 1.7: Archeological survey of INDIA (ASI) uncovered a 5500-year-old (3500 BCE) Harappan city at Dholavira, Gujarat. The city exposed the spectacular hydro-engineering and water management skills of Harappan people.

Illustration 1.8: Rock paintings belong to the Paleolithic period (40000 BCE to 30000 BCE) found in rock caves at Bhimbetka, MP, India (© ASI)

Section – I

(Vedic Astronomy

&

Cradle of Civilization)

2. Vedic Astronomy

"The aforesaid twenty-eight constellations along with the moon may provide peace and happiness to me, so that I may acquire the desired object and be able to keep it intact and may I make the right use of any time all through day and night"

(Atharva Veda 19.8.2)

Geocentric Theory

Vedic Astronomy was built around the assumption that all the heavenly bodies in the Universe revolve around the Pruthvi (Earth). This type of model where the Earth would be the virtual center of the Universe, and Sun, Moon, Nakshatras and other planets revolve around it known as Geo-centric model. The Navagraha (Nine Planets) of Geocentric planetary system consisting of physical bodies such as Ravi (Sun), Soma (Moon), Angaraka (Mars), Sowmya (Mercury), Bruhaspathi (Jupiter), Shani (Saturn), Sukra (Venus), and the logical nodes Rahu (Northern Node) and Ketu (Southern node).

Whereas the modern science believes in Heliocentric model in which earth and planets revolve around the Sun. The Vedic sages knew that the earth is spherical in shape and rotates around the Sun, which is evident from the details found in Vedas. But, for day to day astronomical observations, they assumed Earth as the flat frame of reference from where all the constellations and planets could be viewed. Whereas, the pole star Durva (Polaris) served as the static point of reference for observing the Nakshatras. Thousands of years ago Vedic people noticed that the seasonal changes are due to the movements of Moon, Sun and other celestial bodies such as massive planet Jupiter etc., and its impact on human psychology, so they wanted to give human beings a special position and hence come up with this Geocentric idea where Earth is the center of Universe.

Both the Geo-centric and Heliocentric systems have some merits and de-merits. If you want to measure the distance between Mercury and Sun, the Heliocentric is better. But, if you live inside the arctic circle near the north pole or Antarctic circle near south pole, then the Geo-centric method is more accurate. This lets us to speculate that the Vedic people might observed the heavens from either south pole or from north pole.

Long before Copernicus, Nicolaus (1473 CE - 1543 CE) came up with the heliocentric or sun-centered model, the Yajurveda (Chapter III, verse 6) mentioned about "Earth and its water" moving around the Sun. The famous astronomer of Siddhāntic period, Āryabhata, wrote in his book Āryabhatīya, in year 499 CE, that the stars do not rotate - the earth is the one that rotates around sun. There are many references available in the Vedic literature to confirm that earth is round; for example, the Shatapatha Brahmana (Chapter VII, 1, 1, 37) talks about this. You will find a similar type of references in Kathaka Brahmana, and Jaimini Brahmana. Similarly, several thousands of years ago, long before Newton's theory of gravity published, the Rigveda (VII, 15, 14) and Aitareya Brahmana (I, 23), Kaushitaki Brahmana (chapter VIII, verse 8) and Taittiriya Brahmana (III, 9, 6, 5), all discussed about Earth's gravity, magnetism and the inner crust.

Celestial Sphere

For the purpose of explanation let us use the western terminology to define the Celestial Sphere. If an imaginary sphere is drawn with Earth as the center, as shown in the Illustration 2.1, this imaginary sphere is called as Celestial Sphere. The 'Right Ascension' and 'Declination' used for making astronomical measurements of Nakshatras and Planets within the celestial sphere. It's just like the longitude and latitude define the coordinates of any location on the surface of the Earth. If the South Pole, North Pole and Equator are projected on to the Celestial sphere, they are defined as "South Celestial Pole", "North Celestial Pole" and "Celestial Equator" respectively. The Earth rotates around the Celestial Pole axis from west to east, because of this all the Planets, Constellations and Sun appear to move around Earth from east to west. The points at which Ecliptic intersects with celestial sphere is called equinoxes (Illustration 2.1).

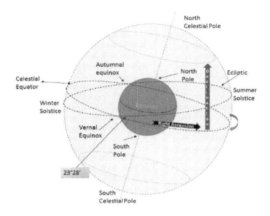

Illustration 2.1: The imaginary Celestial sphere showing Celestial equator, Ecliptic, Equinoxes and Solstices

Precession of the Equinoxes

The Earth is rotating around its celestial pole axis; the orientation of this axis is changing continuously, this shift is about 50 seconds of arc each year or 1° in 72 years. The rate of shift of Earth with respect to the fixed stars (Asterism) is called as the "Rate of Precession". The North Celestial pole is currently pointing towards Polaris and Earth takes almost 26,000 years (to be exact 25,856 years) to make a complete rotation. The star "Vega" becomes the pole star by the year 15000 CE as shown in the illustration 2.2. The current pole star (a star closest to the North Celestial Pole), Polaris, a star in the constellation of Ursa Minor will be replaced by a moderately bright binary star which is located in the constellation of Cepheus, approximately 45 light years from Earth, named Gamma

Cephei (Errai is traditional name derived from Arabic) somewhere around 4000 CE.

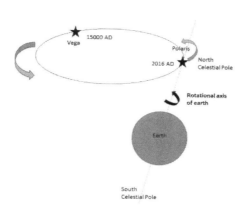

Illustration 2.2: Precession of the Equinoxes

Asterism (Naksatras)

The duration of the sidereal year is 365 days 6 hours 9 minutes and 9.5 seconds. The sidereal year is just over 20 minutes longer than the tropical year with a time difference of 50.26 seconds of celestial longitude. The table 3.1 shows the list of Indian Nakshatras and related constellation, the Taittrīyā Samhitā (2.3.5.1-2.3.5.3) and Rigveda (4.50.4, 10.123.1) talks about the 27 equal parts of the moon's path referring to 27 Nakshatras; the moon takes 27 1/3 days to complete a rotation around earth.

There are 29 ½ days in a lunar month because the Earth moves around itself. So, it takes a couple of days more for the moon to reach the same place on the Earth after completing one rotation. The Rigveda (10.55.3) refers to 34 lights which are Surya (Sun), Soma (Moon), Angaraka (Mars), Sowmya (Mercury), Bruhaspathi (Jupiter), Sukra (Venus), Shani (Saturn) and 27 Nakshatras (it was increased to 28 Nakshatras in the later Vedic texts).

Nakshatra or Star	Other Indian Names (Deity)	Constellation (western Zodiac Name)	Sector (deg, min)
Ashwini	Aswati (Asvinau)	Beta Ariettas	00 00 13 20
Bharani	ApaBharani (Yama)	41 Arietis	13 20 26 40
Karthika	Krithika (Agni)	Eta Tauri	26 40 40 00
Rohini	(Prajapathi)	Alpha Tauri	40 00 53 20
Mrigasara	Mrigashiram (Soma)	Lamda Orionis	53 20 66 40
Aridra	Ardra, Thiruathira (Rudra)	Alpha Orionis	66 40 80 00
Punarvasu	Punarpoosam, Punartham (Aditi)	Beta Geminorum	80 00 93 20
Pushya	Poosam, Pushyami, Pooyam (Brihaspati)	Delta Cancri	93 30 106 40
Aslesha	Asresha, Ayillam (Sarpha)	Alpha Cancri	106 40 120 00
Magha	Makha, Makham, Magam (Pitarah)	Alpha Leonis	120 00 133 20
Purva Phalguni	Pubba, Purva (Baga, Aryaman)	Delta Leonis	133 20 146 40
Uttara Phalguni	Uthiram, Uthram, Uttara (Baga, Aryaman)	Beta Leonis	146 40 160 00

Hasta	Hastham, Atham (Savitar)	Gamma Virgins	160 00 173 20
Chitra	Chittirai, Chitha (Indra)	Alpha Virgins (Spica)	173 20 186 40
Svati	Chothi (Vayu)	Pl Hydrae, Alpha Bootis (Zeta Bootis)	186 40 200 00
Vishaka	Vishakam (Indragni)	Beta Librae	200 00 213 20
Anuradha	Anusham, Anizham (Mitra)	Delta Scorpi	213 20 226 40
Jyeshta	Kettai, Threkettai (Varuna)	Alpha Scorpi	226 40 240 00
Moola	Moolam (Pitarah)	Lamba Scorpi	240 00 253 20
Poorvashad	Puradam, Purva Ashadam (Apah)	Delta Sagittari	253 20 266 40
Utharasad	Utharadam (Visvedevah)	Delta Sagittari	266 40 280 00
Sravana	Shravanam, Chatayam (Visnu	Beta Capricornus	280 00 293 20
(Abhijit)	(Bramha)	Vega	
Dhanishta	Avittam, Dhanishtam (Vasavah)	Alpha Delphini	293 20 306 40
Satabhisha	Sathayam, Chatayam (Varuna)	Lamda Aquar	306 40 320 00
Poorvabhadra	Puruuttahi, Purvabhadr (Aja Ekapad)	Alpha Pegasi	320 00 333 40
Uttarabhadra	Utharadam (Ahirbudhya)	Alpha Andromeda	333 30 346 40
Revati	(Pusan)	Zeta Piscium	346 40 360 00

Table 2.1: Vedic Nakshatras and its related Deity

Vedic Calendar

The ancient Indian calendar was based on the concept of "luni-solar" year system, independently developed by the Dravidian Shiddas, Tribal Priests and Himalayan Sages. At the same time, they also developed a sophisticated method called "Adhika Masa" to synchronize between the lunar and solar years as early as 7000 BCE[1]. The idea of Adhika Masa was mentioned by Varuna in the Rigveda verse 1:25:8. The early Vedic lunar scheme was based on Mukhyamana or Amanta[2] (Amavasya anta) in which the lunar month ends on Amavasya (new-moon); the people in Telangana, Karnataka and Maharashtra still follow this. The New year begins on 'Ugadi', the first day of the bright fortnight of Chaitra Masam.

S. No.	Period	Time frame	Time-keeping Authority
1	Vedic Period	23750 BCE to 8,300 BCE	Sages
2	Puranic Period	8,300 BCE To 3000 BCE	Sages
3	Parashiri Period	3000 BCE To 57 BCE	Priests
4	Varaha Mihira or Siddhantic Period	57 BCE To 1900 CE	Priests
5	Teachers' Period	1900 CE To Present	Priests

Table 2.2: Classification of ancient Indian History by the Telangana Vedic Pundits

Around 285 CE, under the influence of corrupt Buddhist Philosophers, the Sanskrit scholars of north India created a confusion by switching to the Purnimanta (Gaunamana), according to which the month ends on Purnima (full-moon). As per the Purnimanta scheme prevailing in North India, the new year and the beginning of the first lunar month happens at different times. The Vernal Equinox (21 March) was used for the beginning of the new year instead of starting on the winter Solstice, this causes an inaccuracy of 1 day in 72 years even after introducing Adikamasa for sidereal luni-solar correction[3]. The north Indian scheme is a deviation from the Vedic texts, Satapatha Brahmana (SB) 4.3.1.14-19, SB 8.2-8.7 and Taittrīyā Samhita 4.4.11, where the new year and first lunar month begins together after the full-moon.

Based on the Vedic astrological observations, the ancient Indian history can be classified into five eras [4] as shown in the Table-2.2. The demand for Vedic Astrology had led to the major innovations in the mathematics. The Daivajnas (astrologers and priests) used the mathematical equations invented by the Siddhantis. The mathematics replaced the observational astronomy. The ancients predicted the star positions based on the two-dimensional equations with reasonable accuracy. The mathematics helped to predict star positions when not visible during the monsoon seasons. The Jyothisya (Vedic Astrology) has three branches Vedic Astronomy, Ayurveda, and Vastu. In ancient Deccan, the Jyothisya played an important role in the social-economic development. Given below is the partial list of applications where Jyothisya found a place:

- Predicting the monsoon arrivals.
- Determining the festival muhurthams.
- Timeline for planting paddy (rice) and other crop seeds.
- Temple architecture and house construction based on Vastu.
- Scripting the Janma Pathrika for a new born and writing horoscopes etc.

Indian Mathematics predates Greek, Egypt, Chinese or any other ancient civilizations by several thousands of years. For example, the mathematical rules for luni-solar calendar formulated by Sage Lagadha in his Vedanga Jyotish around 1400 BCE, when the Dakshayaniya sacrifices fell short of 5 tithis in the 90-year cycle[3]. After 1100 years, later around 300 BCE, the Babylonians/Sumerians adopted 95-year cycle which was same as the 95-year Agnichayana vidhi described in the Satapatha Brahmana (3000 BCE).This proves that the Babylonians might have adopted it from the Vedic traditions because the Ancient Indians used to have naval trade with Babylonians, Egyptians and Chinese as early as 800 BCE, and India was the first country to pioneer in the ship building and the development of Naval forces.

Table 2.3: Names of Lunar/Jupiter Calendar Years

S No	Varsha	Rasi associated with Jovian Calendar
1	Prabhava	Mesha
2	Vibhava	
3	Sukla	
4	Pramoodotha (Pramoda)	
5	Pajothpatthi (Prajapathi)	
6	Agnirasa	Vrishabha
7	Srimukha	
8	Bhava	
9	Yuva	
10	Dhata (Dhatri)	
11	Eswara	Mithuna

12	Bahudhanya	
13	Pramadi (Pramathin)	
14	Vikrama	
15	Vishu (Vrisha)	
16	Chitrabhanu	Karka
17	Swabhanu (Subhanu)	
18	Tharana	
19	Parthiva	
20	Vyaya	
21	Sarvajittu	Simha
22	Sarvadhari (Sarvadharin)	
23	Virodhi (Virodhin)	
24	Vikriti (Vikrita)	
22	Khara	
26	Nandana	Kanya
27	Vijaya	
28	Jaya	
29	Manmatha	
30	Durmukhi (Durmukha)	
31	Havilambi (Hemalamba)	Tula
32	Vilhambi	
33	Vikari	
34	Sarvari	
35	Plava	
36	Shubhakritu	Vrischika
37	Sobhakruthu (Sobhana)	
38	Krodhi (Krodhin)	
39	Vishwavasu	
40	Paridhavi	

	(Prabhava)	
41	Plavanga	Dhanus
42	Keelaka	
43	Sowmya	
44	Sadharana	
45	Voridhikrutu	
46	Paridhavi	Makara
47	Pramadicha (Pramadin)	
48	Ananda	
49	Rakshasa	
50	Nala (Anala)	
51	Pingala	Kumbha
52	Kalayukti	
53	Siddharthi	
54	Roudri (Raudra)	
55	Durmati	
56	Dunhubhi	Meena
57	Rudhirodgari	
58	Rathakshi	
59	Krodhana	
60	Akshaya (Kshaya)	

The lunar day in a Vedic Calendar is called as a "Tithi", the time it takes for the longitudinal angle between the Moon and Sun to increase by Twelve degrees. There are twelve masa (months) and 60 Samvastsaras (years) in a Vedic Calendar (Table 2.3). The Jovian calendar is also based on 60-year cycle; the time it takes for the planet Jupiter to make five rotations around Sun. The names of the 60 years in both lunar and Jovian Calendars are pretty much same with some minor differences as shown in the table given below, wherever there is a difference the Jovian months are given within the bracket.

The time the Earth takes to move around the Sun is equal to the time Moon rotates around the Earth twelve times, this is called one cycle or one Calendar year. A lunar month has 29.5 days as compared to the 30 days in a solar month. Ancient Hindus used a concept called Adhikamāsam to synchronize between Solar and Lunar Calendars. The solar calendar begins with Sun entering Mesha Rasi (Aries) and ends with Meena Rasi (Pisces). The Rasi is the physical astronomical constellations used in Vedic astronomy as shown in the Table 2.3. The term Nakshatra is also a physical constellation but this is one with which Moon is aligned. The Jupiter based and Lunar based Calendars use the same 60 Varshas as shown in table 2.3. There are some regional variations in India but pretty much all the calendars follow 60-year cycle. In 1940s India used to have more than 6000 types of regional and tribal calendars; even today each and every state, village, and district follow its own calendar along with two other National and Gregorian calendars.

Table-2.4 shows the names of Dravidian & Sanskrit months

List of most popular Lunar and Solar months					
Telugu (Lunar)	Tamil (Solar)	Sanskrit (Lunar)	Malayalam (Solar)	Greek (Solar)	Gregorian (Solar)
Chaitram	Chittrai	Mesha	Medam	Aries	Apr-May
Vaishakam	Vaigasi	Vrishabha	Edaram	Taurus	May-Jun
Jyestam	Ani	Mithuna	Mithunam	Gemini	Jun – July
Ashadam	Adi	Karkata	Karkatakam	Cancer	July-Aug

Shravanam	Avani	Simha	Chingam	Leo	Aug-Sept
Bhadrapadam	Purattasi	Kanya	Kanni	Virgo	Sept-Oct
Aswijam	Alpaisi	Tula	Tulam	Libra	Oct - Nov
Karthikam	Karthigai	Vruschika	Vruschikam	Scorpio	Nov-Dec
Margashiram	Margali	Dhanush	Dhanu	Sagittarius	Dec-Jan
Pushyam	Thai	Makara	Makaram	Capricorn	Jan-Feb
Magham	Masi	Khumba	Kumbham	Aquarius	Feb-Mar
Phalgunam	Panguni	Meena	Meenam	Pisces	Mar-Apr

Based on the semiarid climate of India, the year was divided into six seasons named after the cosmic gods as defined in the Rig-Veda 2.27.1. The six-season calendar was mostly for the chronological and astrological use, but the mainstream population always followed three seasons Rain, Winter and Summer for all practical purposes.

Table 2.5: Names of the Indian seasons

Telugu	Tamil	Sanskrit	Vedic
Vasantha Ruthuvu	Ila-venil	Vasanta	Aryaman
Greeshuma Ruthuvu	Mutu-venil	Grishma	Bhaga
Varsha Ruthuvu	Kaar	Varsha	Varuna
Sharad Ruthuvu	Kulir	Sharada	Daksha
Hemantha Ruthuvu	Mun-pani	Hemanta	Amsha
Sisira Ruthuvu	Pin-pani	Shishira	Mitra

Adhikamāsam during Vedic period

The 19th century Indologist Max Müller, who translated Rgveda, told in his book "Ancient Hindu Astronomy and Chronology, Oxford, 1862", the Vedic 5-year yuga period begins with first year called as Samvatsara, the second year - Parivatsara, third year – Idāvatsara, fourth – Anuvatsara and the fifth year called as Idvatsara.

No. of years (Yugas)	Table 2.6: Adhikamāsa method used in Vedic era			
	Number of days in the 6-year Yuga	Number of days in the Tropical year	Error difference (in days)	Error correction- Extra Adhikamāsa
6 (1)	2190	2191.5	1.5	-
18 (3)	6570	6574.5	4.5	-
23	8400	8400.75	0.75	+1
40	14580 (+30)	14610		+1
*dropped sixth year in 4th & 7th yuga				

As per K.D. Abhyankar, the RV 1-25-8 and Taittrīyā Samhita 3.10.1 gives the names of the six years as Samvatsara, Parivatsara, Idāvatsara, Iduvatsara, Idvatsara and Vatsara[5]. As described in the Atharvaveda (13.3.8), the Adhikamāsa was added after 6 years. The table-2.6 shows how the six year yuga of sidereal year aligns with the Tropical year in 40-years. The Adhikamāsam were added to the 6th year of each yuga and an extra Adhikamāsa needed for the 23rd and 40th year; the 6th year is dropped for the 4th and 7th yuga, at the end of the 40 year both Sidereal (Nakshatra based) and Tropical (Rasi based) years are aligned.

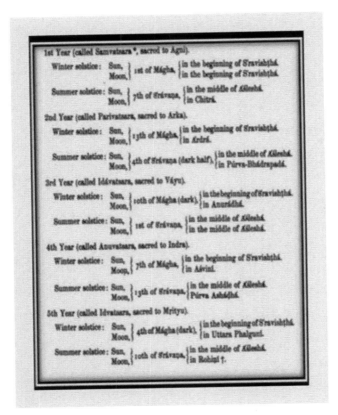

Illustration 2.4: 5-year yuga based on Max Müller's interpretation of Vedas

Adhikamāsam in Ancient Times

The lunar calendar followed in Telangana and other parts of North India will fall short by 11 days (because there are 29.5 days in a lunar month) each year. The ancients noticed this and found a unique way to fix this problem by adding an extra month after every two and half to three years, and they called it **Adhikamāsam**.

Illustration 2.5: Thorlikonda Village Rock fort in the insert (Nizamabad district, Telangana, South Central India); the village once used to be the center for Vedic Pundits during the ancient times. This village is an example on how Adhikamāsam concept was used to synchronize between lunar and solar calendars even in the rural Bharat during the ancient times.

As per the ancient customs prevailing in Thorlikonda and Armoor (Navanathapuram), Nizamabad district, Telangana, the heartland of India (Illustration 2.5), for every two and half years a Adhikamāsam will be added to synchronize the Uttarayanam event (the beginning of the Sun's movement northward for a six-month period) with Makara Sankranti festival and besides this an extra Adhikamāsam will be added after every Twelve years, during the Parvāni celebrations. Sometimes an Adhikamāsam will be deducted if the Amavasya (New Moon) doesn't fall between two Masa-Sankrantees.

Navanathapuram is the old name for Armoor, Nizamabad District, Telangana State, India. As per the legend, during the ancient times Nine Siddhas used to live on top of the hill called "Siddula Gutta", they contributed immensely to the development of panchangam, astrology, Telugu & Sanskrit grammar, and Siddhantas etc. The town was hub for the immigrants from both North and Southern India because of its proximity to an ancient national Highway built by the Pandavas' Chakravarty Yudhistara (present day national High way - NH-7/NH-44) and later renovated by the Emperor Ashoka.

As per the above method of Adhikamāsam calculations, five extra lunar months will be added during the period of Twelve years to synchronize the lunar and solar years. The main expectation during the olden days was to align **Makara Sankranti**, harvest festival with the actual **Uttarayanam** phenomenon after every twelve years. The modern methods are based on Siddhanta Jyothisya and there may be some regional variations on how to calculate the Adhikamāsam, but this concept of 12-year Parvāni was there from the beginning of the time and it was also mentioned in the Mahabharata (Vanaparva – 200-124, 200-125).

"Parvāni dwigunam ... dasagunam bhavet "

Tropical versus Sidereal Zodiac
The Vedic astrology was built around highly advanced and time-tested methods such as Vedic Mathematics, Vedic Astronomy, Ayurveda – a medical branch of Astrology and Vastu – an architectural branch of Vedic Astrology. Whereas Western or Greek astrology built around life and nature concepts. The Vedic astronomy applies the same position of

the Navagraha (Moon, Mars, Mercury, Jupiter, Venus, Saturn, Sun and two logical nodes of Rahu & Ketu) against the background of the fixed heavens (stars), this method called as 'Sidereal Zodiac'. Whereas the western astrology is based on the orientation of the Earth to the Sun, this method is known as 'Tropical Zodiac'. This method assumes that every year, the Sun at the Spring and Autumnal Equinoxes is at first degree of Aries and Libra and for the Summer and Winter Solstices at the first degree of Cancer and Capricorn. There is a fundamental flaw here, in reality the Sun doesn't return to the same position against the background of the fixed stars due to the astronomical phenomenon called 'Precession of the Equinoxes'.

3.   Timeline of Mahabharata war

"Each nation is a Shakti or power of the evolving spirit … the Bharata Shakti, the living energy of a great spiritual conception … For by its virtue alone she has been one of the immortal nations … the secret of her amazing persistence and perpetual force of survival and revival"

-SRI AUROBINDO

(in his book "The foundations of the Indian culture", 1953)

Mahabharata Chronology

Oct 13, 3138 BCE	Balarama sets off on yatra on the banks of Sarasvatī river. He started on the Pushya Nakshatra
Nov 6, 3138 BCE	Mahabharata war begins at Kurukshetra
Nov 24, 3138 BCE	Balarama returns from Sarasvatī yatra on Shravana Nakshatra, the day Mahabharata war ended
3102 BCE	Beginning of **Kali Yuga** (based on astronomical references) on March **22, 3102, Sunday, 2 hours 27 minutes 30 seconds in** the afternoon. When all the seven planets (Sun, Moon, Mars, Mercury, Venus, Jupiter, and Saturn) were aligned near Makara Rasi as defined in the Puranic Sutras. The Uranus and Pluto were aligned too, but not counted as planets as per Vedic Astronomy.

When did Kali Yuga begin?

The Mahabharata war was the last time when the Gods, Asuras and Men roamed together the planet Earth. Based on the writings of the great sages of Himalayas Narada and Veda Vyasa, the Gods were the human manifestations of Indra, Krishna and Sankara. The Asuras were the Ghatotkacha (son of Pandavas prince Bhīma & the demon Hidimbhi) and his Asura army. The dateline of Mahabharata is the gateway to the history of Ancient India and the world. More than 50 kingdoms and 16 Mahajanapadas of Bharata participated in the Mahabharata war. As per the ancient Indian records, the Kali yuga occurred 36 years after the Mahabharata War.

Based on both Vedic and Puranic traditions, the Kali Yuga might have begun on Sunday, the first day of Chaitra Masam around 2 hours 27 minutes 30 seconds in the afternoon at Ujjain, India. Which is nothing but the Ugadi, the beginning of the new Era, when the Seven planets were aligned on a straight line near Makara Rashi, a rare event occurs after more than 4 million years. Using astronomy software, I recalculated the beginning of Kali Yuga to March 22, 3102, Sun day, the first day of Chaitra Masam around 2 hours 27 minutes 30 seconds in the afternoon at Ujjain, India. This was the time when all the Seven planets (Geocentric model) Sun, Moon, Mercury, Venus, Jupiter, and Saturn were aligned near Makara Rashi. Puranic sages might have used either specialized astronomical instruments or the mathematical equations to calculate the Kaliyuga event. Even if they didn't use any observational astronomic Instruments or mathematical equations, the Planet alignment near Makara Rasi would be still visible to a naked eye whenever a passing cloud blocks the sun, as shown in the screen-shots of Astronomy simulation (Illustrations 3.1 and 3.2).

The Kaliyuga occurred on either on Wednesday Feb 18, 3102 BCE or Friday Feb 20, 3102 BCE, according to the   Western and Indian historians. They were correct about the year, but wrong about the month and day. The difference might be due to the delta between Gregorian and Julian calendars. Since the Mahabharata occurred 36 years before the beginning of Kali Yuga, the time of Mahabharata war must be the year 3138 BCE.

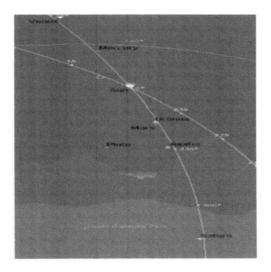

Illustration 3.1: Simulation based on the Astronomy software uncovered a rare celestial event of Seven Planet alignment on Kali Yuga day, Mar 22, 3102 BCE; at Ujjain, MP, India around 2:27:30 PM (from top to bottom: Venus, Mercury, Moon, Sun, Mars, Jupiter and Saturn; Pluto and Uranus also seen aligned but not counted in the Vedic astronomy)

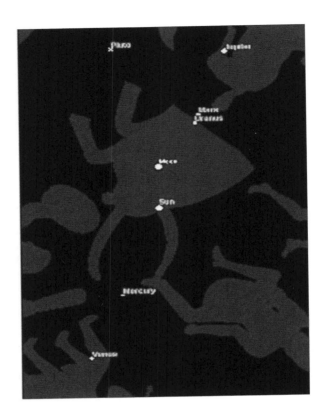

Illustration 3.2: Another simulated view of the Seven Planet alignment on the first day of the beginning of the Kali Yuga Era near Makara Rashi (shown in the background) on Sun day, the first day of Chaitra Masam (March 22, 3102BCE, 2:27 PM, Ujjain, MP, India). From bottom to top: Venus, Mercury, Sun, Moon, Jupiter, Mars, and Saturn; Pluto and Uranus also seen aligned but not counted in the Vedic astronomy

Date of Mahabharata based on inscriptions

The date of Mahabharata was mentioned in the riddle like inscription located at Jain Temple, Aihole (Karnataka, India). This was constructed by the famous Chalkuya King Pulakeshi-II in the year 634 CE. It reads as follows:

Trinshatsu Trisahasreshu Bhaaratha Dahavaditaha|
Saptabda Shatayukteshu Gateshwabdeshu Panchasu|
Panchashatasu Kalaukale Shatasu Panchashatsu cha|
Samatsu Samatitasu Shakaanamamapi Bhoobhujaam||

There might be an error in the inscription or a few words changed over the period, so the inscription doesn't make sense. For calculation purpose let us use **Ghatasu** instead of Shatasu as suggested in the ancient historical records (1892-1903) – 'The Prachina-lekha-mala'. After modification, the inscription reads as follows:

Trinshatsu Trisahasreshu Bhaaratha Dahavaditaha |
Saptabda Shatayukteshu Gateshwabdeshu Panchasu |
Panchashatasu Kalaukale Ghatasu Panchashatsu cha |
Samatsu Samatitasu Shakaanamamapi Bhoobhujaam ||

Many scholars seem to disagree with this inscription because of the confusion on which Shaka era to use. The word "Shakaanamamapi Bhoobhujaam" on the fourth line of the inscription referring to a king who killed more number of Shakas[2]. Based on the ancient history books and inscriptions the emperor Shalivana's army was responsible for killing a large number of Shakas in a war and hence the dispute about which Shaka era is resolved forever. The inscription says temple was constructed 556 years after Shaka era, and 30 (Trinshatsu) + Trisahasreshu (3000) + 700 + 5 (Panchasu), which is equal to 3735 years from Kali Era. Considering the 78 A.D. (78 CE) as the Salivahana Saka, the temple was built in 634 CE (556+78). Similarly, considering 36 years passed between Mahabharata and Kaliyuga Era and 633 years in the

Shaka Era; the inscription says the Mahabharata war happened in the year **3136** BCE[3] (3735 +36 -633). Several scholars used 634 years for calculation, which is wrong, there is no 0CE (0 AD) or 0 BCE (OBC), so it must be 633 years.

Table 3.1: Genealogy of ancient kings

Name of the Dynasty	No. of Kings	No. of years reigned
Barhadradha	22	1006
Pradhyota	5	138
Nagas	10	360
Nandas	9	100
Mauryas	12	316
Sungas	10	300
Kanwas	4	85
Satavahana	32	506
Total		2811

Time of Mahabharata 2811 + 327 = 3138 BCE

We crossed three firewalls, first one between Julian and Gregorian Calendar methods, the second between 1BCE and 1CE and the third between the Kaliyuga and Twilight zone of Dwapara-Kaliyuga. We should take this into consideration when calculating the time of Mahabharata. Without taking the above mentioned three firewalls into account the Mahabharata year is 3136 BCE. There is a difference of 796 days, if I follow the calculations of western astronomer Bentley and taking into consideration all the three firewall differences. This is because of the difference between two types of Calendars in existence in the past. The first type used Magha masa as the beginning of the year during the Mahabharata time, and the Second type used the Chaitra masa as the beginning of the year from the start of Kaliyuga. But the astronomy software shows an additional 30-day difference, probably due to the delta between the Gregorian and Julian Calendars, hence the total difference should be 826 days or 2.26 years. This brings the date of Mahabharata to the either   3138.18 (3136 + 2.18) years before Christ (BCE) based on Bentley Method, or 3138.26 (3135 + 2.26) years before Christ based on the astronomy software, hence the year **3138 BCE** is the time of Mahabharata war.

Based on Ancient Hindu History

Despite so many catastrophes, the ancient Indians kept the genealogy records of Kings very well. The Kaliyuga Raja Vrittanta Purana has the details of the ancient kings from the beginning of Mahabharata war and up to the end of Satavahana dynasty in 327 BCE. The Satavahana dynasty also called as Telugu dynasty, when the dynasty was at its peak, the territory consisting of present day Telangana State, four South Indian states, and parts of Deccan which includes Maharashtra, Madhya Pradesh and Orissa. According to the table **3.1**, the Barhadradha dynasty lasted for 1006 years, Pradhyota for 138 years, Nagas for 360 years, Nanda dynasty for 100, Mauryas for 316 years, Sungas 300 years, Kanwas for 85 years and Andhra dynasty ruled for 506 years. Based on the Ancient Indian Puranic Chronology the Mahabharata occurred in the year **3138 BCE** and the Kaliyuga, the beginning of a new era happened in the year **3102 BCE**.

4. A New Theory On Cradle of Civilization

"O Supreme Lord, grant me that Vision

Which the ancient sages were endowed with,

And which made them divine"

(Atharva Veda 6.108.4)

Truth in Arctic home in the Vedas?

The Vedic era Mount Meru plays an important role in finding the original home of Vedic hymns, which is nothing but the Cradle of civilization. Many European scholars asserted that the Arctic circle was the home of Vedic Aryans. They based their opinion on the then accepted Aryan Invasion theory (AIT). Both 20th Century and 21st Century scholars have already rejected the AIT. There was not enough archeological evidence found to substantiate the Aryan Invasion theory any way. DNA evidence concluded that the Vedic Cows were of Indian origin[1]. Most of the cows and rats migrated from India and reached all six continents in the world today. At least, this makes us to rethink that India might be the birth place of Aryans.

During the Glacial period around 10,000 BCE, no one survived in the arctic circle near north pole. The lack of evidence disqualifies the views of the Sri Bala Gangadhar Tilak and European researchers on the Arctic concept. On the other hand, the work of Sri Bala Gangadhar Tilak's High Chronology theory that moved the antiquity of Vedas by 6000 years, serves as the starting point for a new investigation on the origin of Aryan home. We now have several references in the post-Vedic texts which prove that the Aryans might have entered India well before 7500 BCE.

Aryan Reverse Migration Theory (ARMT)
As per my newly proposed Theory:

"The cradle of civilization is India, and the Aryans were of Indian origin. The people migrated from India towards Australia, Americas, Europe and Kumari Kandam (lost continent in South Indian Ocean) between 83,000 BCE and 43,000 BCE. The combination of plate techonomic activity and loss of gravity created millions of submarine volcanos in the south Indian Ocean. As the result of which the whole continent, Kumari Kandam, started sinking into the Indian Ocean. This prompted the reverse migration of Indo-European races towards Indian subcontinent. This took place sometime between 30,000 BCE and 5500 BCE. Some of the Aryans (fair-skinned Indo-Aryans, now called as Brahmins) stayed back in India but other Indo-European races such as Celt, Teuton, Greek, Iranian, Vend, the Lett and Latin went towards Europe, Middle East, North America, and central Asia. These races no longer exist in present day, but the people can be found in the countries like Russia, Britain, France, Germany, Canada and United States etc. The first mount Meru was probably in the Antarctic circle, near south pole not the Arctic circle as predicted by some. The planet Uranus is not visible from south pole most of the days in a year. That might be the reason why the Uranus was not part of the Vedic Astronomy. The Kumari Kandam was the home to the first river-valley Vedic culture, after the Kumari Kandam lost gravity and sunk into Indian Ocean, the Vedic River Culture (VRC) continued on the Banks of Sapta Sindhavah – Godavari, Cauvery, Tungabhadra, Narmadā, Yamuna, Ganga and Sarasvatī".

The migration of people from mainland India occurred between 83,000 BCE and 43,000 BCE. They went into three directions. The first batch went towards Kumari Kandam (some people might call it as an ancient alien civilization) in the direction of south Indian Ocean. The other two batches went towards Australia and Madagascar and finally ended up in the Kumari Kandam. Several 19th Century scholars speculated about the cradle of civilization, the lost continent Lemuria or Mu. But, they searched elsewhere in Pacific Ocean instead of South Indian Ocean.

Based on the geological records, the worst glacial phase occurred between 75,000 BCE and 65,000 BCE. During this period the world population entirely whipped out. The only exceptions were India,

Kumari Kandam, Southeast Asia and East Africa. Similarly, no one survived in China, but the current Han population came from Northeast India around 40,000 BCE. In the post-glacial era, the culture continuity in the Kumari Kandam led to the evolution of many Indo-European languages and races. The series of deluges forced the Indo-European to migrate towards mother India. They first arrived in south India in several batches between 30,000 BCE and 5500 BCE (Illustration 4.1). In the beginning, they might have used water buffalos, whales and other water born animals to cross the ocean. Later, they built the ships and used the ancient navigation methods. It may not be possible to provide any archeological evidence with the existing technologies. The South Indian Ocean where the Kumari Kandam continent submerged is surrounded by a large number of active volcanos, and it poses a serious challenge to any underwater archeological activity. Per latest reports there are around 10 million sub-marine volcanos exist in the world and most of these active volcanoes are situated in the south Indian ocean.

The ancient habitat of Tamil people was part of the "JAMBU THEEVU". This was mentioned in the Tamil puranic Manimekalai (section XI.107). Which is nothing but the lost continent Lemuria or Kumari Kandam. Per Tamil sources, the continent was named after the river Kumari. This proves the existence of Kumari-Kandam river-valley culture precursor to Sarasvatī-Indus valley culture. The proto-Tamil has genetic relationship with all other Indo-European languages. This was mentioned by the Thiru Sattur Sekaran, a Tamil linguist. Which confirms the co-existence of Tamil and Indo-European civilization in the Kumari Kandam.

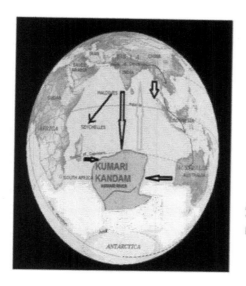
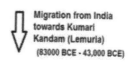
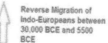

Migration from India towards Kumari Kandam (Lemuria) (83000 BCE - 43,000 BCE)

Reverse Migration of Indo-Europeans between 30,000 BCE and 5500 BCE

A REVERSE IMMIGRATION THEORY ON ORIGIN OF INDO-EUROPEAN RACE

Illustration 4.1: A theory on Aryan Migration to and from India and Lost continent Kumari Kandam (lost continent in the South Indian Ocean; that may be the reason Aryans considered South as the land of Demons)

The people from mainland India migrated between 83,000 BCE and 43,000 BCE in different directions and finally reached Kumari Kandam. This has been confirmed by the DNA lineage migration, India responsible for the Paternal Lineage C and D, and the Maternal Lineage M. The Indian origin of Paternal haplogroup R1a1* shows that the Indo-Europeans originated in India[1]. Aryans called South as the land of Yama (or Lord of Death) because their original home Kumari Kandam, near Antarctic circle submerged into the South Indian ocean.

Section – II

(Gods & Goddesses)

5. Goddess Sarasvatī

Ambitame

Naditame

Devitame

-Rigveda

(Best of Mothers, Best of rivers, Best of Goddesses)

Chronology

30,000 BCE - 5500 BCE	Aryan (Indo-European) immigration into North India and South India through seven river mouths via sea routes. The Aryans initially took-up the agriculture jobs, but later the Kshatriyas (ruling class) introduced them to Vedas. Existence of Mighty mystic perennial river Vedic Sarasvatī.
7000 BCE- 1900 BCE	Existence of urban Vedic Sarasvatī Civilization. Most of the Vedas were already composed and Sages recited Vedic hymns on the banks of mighty Sarasvatī river.
4000 BCE – 3000 BCE	Sarasvatī lost its perennial status presumably due to the plate tectonic activity. The RADARSAT paleo-channel (PC) image delineated (Figure 5.8) rivers Yamuna and Sutlej as the major contributors to the mighty waters of Vedic Saraswati. After major earthquake, the present day river Sutlej moved westwards and separated from Sarasvatī'. At the same time another major perennial source drifted away eastwards and merged into the present-day river Yamuna. So, **Gangotri steals Sarasvatī via Yamunotri.**

Oct 13, 3138 BCE	Balarama sets off on Sarasvatī river yatra on Pushya Nakshatra.
Nov 6, 3138 BCE	Mahabharata war began at Kurukshetra[1].
Nov 24, 3138 BCE	Balarama returned from Sarasvatī yatra on Shravana Nakshatra, the day Mahabharata war ended.
3000 BCE – 1950 BCE	Earth quakes in the Himalayan region followed by Twelve-year continuous drought completely wiped out the flora and fauna; dried up the Sarasvatī basin and paved the way to the desert formation (Present day Gobi Desert).
1900 BCE	Vedic River Sarasvatī completely dried up.
Nov, 1985 CE	**Akil Bharatiya Itihas Sankalan Samiti** and the prominent Indian Historian **Dr. Vishnu S. Wakankar** along with senior RSS (Rashtriya swayam sevak) pracharak **Moropant Pingale** launched "**Vedic Sarasvatī River Expedition**" in search of the lost Vedic river.

River Goddess

The **Goddess Sarasvatī**, also spelled as **Saraswati** meaning 'the flowing one' or 'watery'. She is also the goddess of knowledge, divine inspiration, music, speech, science and arts. The mythical river Sarasvatī was once considered the most sacred rivers of north-western India. During the Vedic period the river Sarasvatī was an important river for irrigation and transportation purposes. The most advanced civilization did exist on the banks of this Vedic river (present day, Gagger). Based on the geological evidence, the river was so mighty with 34 kilometers wide, the area of irrigation equal to one fourth of India's fertile land before it was merged into the sea at Rann of Kutch.

The river dried up due to the plate tectonic activity occurred in the Himalayan basin. The Sarasvatī river lost its course and merged into the Yamunotri (River Yamuna) near its perennial source in the Himalayas. Because of this plate tectonic activity, the flow of water had become intermittent. The RADARSAT paleo-channel (PC) image delineated (Figure 5.8) rivers Yamuna and Sutlej as the major contributors to the mighty waters of Vedic Saraswati. After major earthquake, the present day river Sutlej moved westwards and separated from Sarasvatī'. At the same time another major perennial source drifted away eastwards and merged into the present-day river Yamuna.

Since the river Sarasvatī lost its perennial status, it flowed only whenever there was a rain. This activity continued for a few more thousand years and at the end river dried up completely due to the 12-year persisting drought. The Sarasvatī river disappears into the dunes of sand at Vinashena (near Patiala, Punjab). These historical references were made in the Mahabharata and other Puranic texts. As per the legend, the Sarasvatī river flows underground and merges into Ganga. This mythology actually referring to the real historical account of

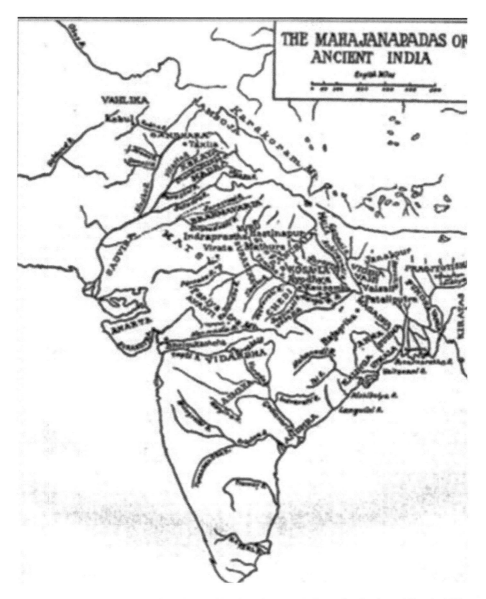

Illustration 5.1: The map of ancient India, river Sarasvatī shown in the dotted line (©ASI)

geological phenomenon caused by plate tectonic activity. The Sages believed that the Saraswati river might be flowing underground and merging with rivers Ganga and Yamuna. The merger of Sarasvatī into

Yamuna occurs at Himalayas and the merger of Yamuna and Ganga happening at Prayaga (present day Allahabad, Uttar Pradesh, India). The Sages named this place as the 'Triveni Sangam', because the three rivers (Ganga, Yamuna and invisible Sarasvati) merged here. The 7th century Emperor and Sanskrit scholar Harshavardhana (590 CE - 648 CE) started Khumba Mela at Triveni Sangam. The Khumba Mela is a sacred river bath to cleanse all the sins. More than 100 million people take part in Khumba Mela and this event occurs once in every twelve years.

The illustration 5.3 is an artistic view of the mighty river Sarasvati merging into Arabian sea. The river Sarasvati might have disappeared but the Goddess Sarasvati still permeates the minds of millions of Indians (Illustration 5.2). Even today people of India celebrate "Vasant Panchami", the 5th day of spring, in her honor. The young children undergo "Aakshara Abyasam" in several parts of India, an initiation of writing alphabets before they are admitted to preschool or nursery school.

Goddess of Divine Inspiration

Per the Indian nationalist and mystic philosopher Sri Aurobindo (1872-1950), wrote in his book "The secret of the Veda", 1950 (first published in the monthly review Arya 1914-20):

"The symbolism of the Veda betrays itself with the greatest clearness in the figure of the goddess Sarasvati. In many of the other gods the balance of the internal sense and the external figure is carefully preserved. The veil sometimes becomes transparent or its corners are lifted even for the ordinary hearer of the Word; but it is never entirely removed. One may doubt

Illustration 5.2: Goddess Sarasvatī, one hand holding Vedas, signifying the mother of Vedas, the other hands playing Veena – representing the goddess of music.

Illustration 5.3: Ancient imaginary map of Vedic Sarasvatī, around 8000 BCE
(Source: Lost River)

whether Agni is anything more than personification of the sacrificial Fire or the physical principle of the Light and Heat in things, or Indra anything more than the god of the sky and the rain and or of physical Light, or Vayu anything more than the divinity in the Wind and Air or at most of the physical life-breath. In the lesser gods, the naturalistic interpretation has less ground for confidence; for it is obvious that Varuna is not merely a Vedic

Uranus or Neptune, but a god with great and important moral functions; Mitra and Bhaga have the psychological aspect; the Ribhus who form things by the mind and build up immortality by works can with difficulty be crushed into the Procrustean measure of a naturalistic mythology. Still by imputing a chaotic confusion of ideas to the poets of the Vedic hymn the difficulty can be trampled upon, if not overcome. But Sarasvatī will submit to no such treatment. She is, plainly and clearly, the goddess of the Word, the goddess of a divine Inspiration. "

The goddess Sarasvatī mentioned in Vedas as the most powerful feminine deity as well as the mystic river (that disappeared around 1900 BCE). According to the Rigveda (1.3.12), she imparts deep knowledge to all who are seekers of the truth and knowledge. The goddess Sarasvatī also known as Savitri (meaning "descended from the Sun"), Brahmani (power of Brahma), Brahmi (goddess of sciences), Vani (goddess of music), Varnesvari (goddess of letters), Sharada (one who loves the autumn season), Chaduvula Thalli (in Telugu, goddess of knowledge), Kalaimagal (in Tamil), and Gayatri (Mother of Vedas). Sarasvatī is also revered as the goddess of great inspiration, music, knowledge, and arts by several believers outside India and Nepal such as Japan, Vietnam, Indonesia (Bali), Myanmar, United Kingdom, United States, Australia, and New Zealand. The Gnana Sarasvatī temple, one of the most famous temples of Goddess Sarasvatī, is located on the banks of the magnificent river Godavari at Basar Village, Telangana (Illustration 5.4). As per the legends the original temple was constructed by Veda Vyas somewhere around 3100 BCE. The temple was later renovated in 6th Century CE by a Karnataka King named Bijialudu, who ruled Nandagiri, a village in Telangana.

Illustration 5.4: Gnana Sarasvatī Temple, Basar, Telangana

Illustration 5.5: World's first Vedic Sila, precursor to Goddess Sarasvatī's Veena, located at Basar, Telangana, India

Shapta Sargam

The Veda Sila (Vedic Stone) located at the Basar village, Telangana on the banks of Godavari. It was built by the Vedic sages several thousands of years ago, one of its kind in the entire world. This is an ancient musical stone instrument that generates the Shapta Saralu (7 notes). The seven notes are Sa, Re Ga, Ma, Pa, Da, and Ni. This granite stone instrument is a precursor to the Goddess Sarasvatī's musical instrument Veena. This granite rock musical structure is located on the banks of majestic Godavari river, near Sarasvatī temple, Basra Village (Illustration 5.5), Telangana.

Balarama Tirthayatra

The Mahabharata has many references to the Vedic river Sarasvatī, out of which the Tirthayatra of Balarama is of a special interest on a historical point of view. To avoid Mahabharata war, Balarama, the elder brother of Sri Krishna, comes up with an excellent excuse in the name of Sarasvatī Tirthayatra. The Shalya Parva (proceedings of the 18th day of Mahabharata war on which Shalya becomes the supreme commander of the Kauravas army) has the following Sanskrit reference:

चत्वारिंशदहान्यद्य द्वे च मे निः सृतस्य वै
पुष्येण संप्रयातो स्मि श्रवणे पुनरागतः

The meaning is as follows:

"I left for yatra on Pushya Nakshatra and returning back on Shravana Nakshatra, after 42 days"

The Mahabharata describes 'Kurukshetra', the place where the Mahabharata war occurred (250 square kilometer area) as the land south of Sarasvati and north of Drishtavati (Drishadvati) rivers. Balarama started from a place called Prabhasa (a tīrtha, what is called as Somnath in Sauraushtra) and went upstream towards the East and reached hundreds of tīrthas and a big unknown city where he bought cows, jewels, pearls, and horses from foreign traders, etc. to distribute these to the Brahmins. Balarama noticed the river vanishing (based on the descriptions of Shalya Parva section 36 & 37) at the place called Udapana, but the farmers recognized the underground existence of the river based on the wet condition and the soil moisture.

Illustration 5.6: A map of the 'Sapta-Sindhou' published in 1881 French book 'Vedic India'. The map adds the rivers with names in Sanskrit and Greek, Sarasvatī identified with the Ghaggar and located between the Yamuna and the Sutlej.

Sapta-Sindhavah (Seven Rivers)

The Rig Veda speaks constantly about seven rivers, but due to the lack of clarity of explanation, no one really knows how it needs to be enumerated. As per the book published in France in the year 1881 CE, **Vedic India**, included a map of the Land of Seven Rivers (as shown in illustration 5.6), the Sarasvatī was identified with present day Ghaggar and located between the Yamuna and the Sutlej. The Sapta-Sindhavah can be identified with Sarasvatī in the east, and the Sindhu in the west and five rivers Satudru, Vipasa, Asikini, Parusni (Iravati) and Vitasta. All these rivers have the male names and not sure how it can be called as the sisters of Sarasvatī. For example, Asikini real name is Chenab; the modern name of Vitasta is Jhelum; Sindhu is nothing but Indus, another male name; Vipasa is Beas, Satudru is Sutlej and Parusni or Iravati is Ravi. So, the search for the Sapta-Sindhavah doesn't stop here, it must be continued until it makes sense.

According to the British scholar, an authority on Asian civilization, Arthur L. Bhasam, the Vedic description of Sapta-Sindhavah was limited to a small region. He wrote in his famous book "Wonder That Was India" as follows:

"When the [Rig Vedic] hymns written the focus of Âryan culture was the region between Jamnā (Sanskrit Yamunā) and Sutlej (Shutudri), south of the modern Ambālā, and along the upper course of the river Sarasvatī. The later river is now insignificant stream, losing itself in the desert of Rajasthan, but it then [in Rig Vedic times] flowed broad and strong, and probably joined the Indus below the confluence of Satlaj. The Vedic poets knew the Himālayas, but not the land south of the jamnā, and they didn't mention Vindhyas …"

As per Dr. V.S. Wakankar, more than 40 Vedic Seers from south of Vindhyas belonging to various schools of Vishwamitra, Bhardwaj,

Kanwa, Atri and Angiras (complete list of names given in the Appendix-II) participated in the composition of Vedic Hymns[1]. The Valmiki mentioned in his book Ramayana that the Lanka King Ravana was well versed in Vedas. Therefore, the Aryan culture was not just limited to the Indus-Punjab area; the Vedas originated originally in the South of Vindhyas and later Sarasvatī became the center of Vedic civilization because Southern India had been hit with series of deluges in the years 16,000 BCE, 14056 BCE, 9564 BCE, 2939 BCE, 2387 BCE and 1715 BCE. So, it's pretty clear the Vedic seers probably didn't mean Sapta-Sindhavah as the Indus and nearby rivers instead the mighty southern rivers of India.

Proof of existence of Mythical River Saraswati

In the year 1985 CE, Akil Bharatiya Itihas Sankalan Samiti and the prominent Indian Historian Dr. Vishnu S. Wakankar along with senior RSS (Rashtriya swayam sevak) pracharak Moropant Pingale launched "Vedic Sarasvatī River Expedition" in search of the lost Vedic river. The remote sensing data and LANDSAT imaginary uncovered the paleo-channels of the lost Vedic river and its tributaries (Illustration 5.8), which paved a way to the re-birth of Sarasvatī.

The Indian newspapers reported as follows: "under the pressure of the left-wing ideologues the government of India denounced this expedition as a myth in the beginning ..." At last, it was a stunning victory as the Indian government now agrees to revive the VEDIC river which was lost several thousands of years back. Per the news published in the Indian express, dated March 2, 2016, according to the India's Minister of water resources Ms. Uma Bharathi, the government has decided to constitute an expert committee headed by Prof K.S. Vaidya, a former vice-chancellor of Kumoan University to find out if the

LANDSAT and the other exploration data is indeed related to the Sarasvatī river.

Illustration 5.8: Digital image processing (simplified view) of IRS-P6 AWiFS and Radarsat SAR images revealing the existence of Sarasvatī river (blue channels) between 28000 BCE and 5000 BCE (courtesy: Regional Remote Sensing Centre, Department of Space, Govt. of India, Jodhpur, Rajasthan, India); the simplified view of paleo channels from Mansarovar lake in the Himalayas to mythical city Dwaraka.

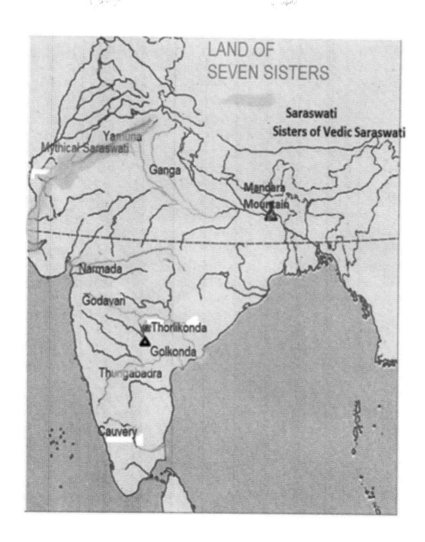

Illustration 5.7: Newly proposed the Land of Seven Rivers

A New Theory - The Land of Seven Rivers (Sapta-Sindhavah)

According to the new theory I am proposing the land of seven rivers are not the rivers of Punjab but the "River system of India" as mentioned in Rig-Veda. Based on epics, the Punjab is known as the land of five rivers. In one form or other the Vedas are still alive in the everyday lives of millions of Indians. For example, the Gayatri Mantra, the people recite this all the time without knowing that it's a Vedic scripture. Vishwamitra compiled Gayatri Mantra and hymns of Rig-Veda on the banks of Godavari. Does the Sapta Sindhavah mean the seven mouths of Godavari merging into the Ocean?

Name of the River	Origin	Termination
Sarasvatī (Mighty river till 4000BCE, completely dried up around 1900 BCE)	Himalayas	Rann of Kutch, Arabian Sea
Godavari	Trimbak, Deccan Plateau	Bay of Bengal
Tungabhadra		Bay of Bengal
Cauvery	Talakaveri, Western Ghats	Bay of Bengal
Ganga	Himalayas	Bay of Bengal
Narmada	Narmada Kund, Madhya Pradesh	Gulf of Khambat, Arabian Sea
Yamuna	Yamunotri, Utterkhand	Bay of Bengal

Table 5.1: Newly proposed Sapta-Sindhavah by the author

The Indo-Europeans (Aryans) entered India through the river mouths of seven rivers (Sapta-Sindhavah) Godavari, Ganga, Tungabhadra, Cauvery, Narmada, Yamuna and Sarasvatī via sea routes. Rigveda (Rig. 1.72.8) clearly states[3] "They found the Seven rivers and thereby discovered the doors of prosperity. Saramā found the stolen cows and the Mankind got its Food". The Aryans found the cows and started the agriculture in the beginning. The Vedic Sages built the Hermitage and recited Vedas on the banks of major southern rivers. Later, the banks of Sarasvatī became the center of Vedic civilization.

The Sages migrated towards north to escape from the series of deluges occurring in South. The Vedas mentioned, the Gods are in constant battle with Asuras. To give the human beings the mighty river waters flow into the sea. The seven sisters can't be the tributaries of Sarasvatī, but the River System of ancient India whose river mouths merge into the ocean. The list of newly proposed **Sapta-Sindhavah** (Seven rivers, Illustration 5.7) is given in the table 5.1. Indo-Aryans and Indo-Europeans migrated into India through the river mouths of the **Sapta-Sindhavah** (above mentioned seven rivers) sometime between 30,000 BCE and 5,000 BCE, please refer to the chapter-4 on new reverse migration theory of Aryans.

6. Supreme God Vishnu

"Non-violence is the greatest force at the disposal of mankind, it is mightier than the mightiest weapon of destruction devised by the ingenuity of man"

-Mahatma Gandhi

(An unofficial reincarnation of Lord Vishnu; who fought against evil British empire and threw them out of India using his innovative non-violence technique called "Satya Graham")

Vedic Chronology

23000 BCE – 17000 BCE   Lord Vishnu, the first Dravidian astronomer lived sometime during this period. The Vedic sages initially assigned a small planet Mercury to honor the Vamana avatar. But, later on Lord Vishnu became one of the three greatest deities (Shiva and Shakti are the other two) of Puranic Traditions.

11,000 BCE   Samudra Manthan by Gods (Devas) and anti-Gods (Asuras); the knowledge transfer of Vedas and Ayurveda by the Dravidian Shiddas to the Himalayan Rishis at the mount Mandara (West Bihar, India)

7500 BCE - 7400 BCE   Kshatriya King turned Sage Vishvamitra introduced the new time reference where Sravana being the first Nakshatra at Autumnal Equinox.

7000 BCE   Vedic Astronomers[1] came up with a unique concept of Adhikamāsam to synchronize between lunar and solar years.

3138 BCE   Lord Krishna, an incarnation of Lord Vishnu, gave sermon in the battle field of Kurukshetra to the Pandavas princess and great warrior Arjuna, who was reluctant to fight with his cousins, relatives and friends. The sermon of Lord Krishna collectively called as Sacred Bhagavad-Gita (combination of Bhakti Yoga, Karma Yoga, Jnana Yoga and Maya Yoga)

3102 BCE

Beginning of Kaliyuga; Lord Krishna passed away in the same year, marking the end of Dwapara Yuga.

1100 CE

Ramanuja develops a qualified system of Monism called 'Visishtadvaita'

1824CE - 1883CE

Dayananda Sarasvatī, the Hindu religious reformer, founder of Arya Samaj lived during this period.

1875 CE

Swami Dayananda Sarasvatī forms Arya Samaj.

1869 CE – 1948 CE

Mohandas Karamchand **Gandhi** (India's father of the nation) lived during this period, who almost single handedly kicked out British Empire from India. Gandhi, a potential candidate for Lord Vishnu's reincarnation, should there be an extension of Dashavatara (10 incarnations) to Solavatara (16 incarnations). Gandhiji translated the Sanskrit version of Bhagvad Gita to English language to unite 400 Million Hindus for his "Satyagraha" (Non-Violent) movement against British.

1863 CE – 1902 CE

Vivekananda, a key figure in revival of Hinduism at the world arena. His famous speech at the world parliament of Religions at Chicago in 1893 completely changed the western perception of Hinduism.

Vishnu Anantashayana

As per the Sattva Puranas (Vishnu Purana, Bhagavata Purana, and Brahma Valvarta Purana), Vishnu is the Supreme God who creates an unlimited number of universes (multiverses) and enters each one of them in the form of Avatar as the preserver of the world to redress the balance between good and evil. There is a clear distinction between the Brahma, the creator within the Universe and the Vishnu, the creator of the multiverse. As per the Hindu traditions, the God Vishnu is situated in the "**Makara Rashi**" and some others consider Vishnu's eye is situated at the infinitely long distant, Southern Celestial Pole.

The creation of Vishnu Avatars was undoubtedly the greatest idea ever come to the minds of the Himalayan Sages. The Vedic Sages were just the architects of the Vedas and other Vedic texts but not the worriers. To protect themselves from the aggressive Asuras they needed the help of Kings and Emperors. So, the Puranic Sages came up with a unique scheme of Avatars where they mix up the un-manifested God Vishnu with the real-world warriors who could prevail the truth and protect the society. On a philosophical level the Avatars are the symbolic representation of evolution of life. The illustration 6.1 is the rock sculpture of Vishnu Anantashayana (Ananta means infinite) depicting the cosmic process of creation, preservation and destruction of the Universe. The creation process begins as soon as Vishnu resting on the coils of Naga Seshu which is floating in the Pala-Samudram (cosmic ocean). Vishu awakes from Yoganidra, the lotus sprouts from his naval, revealing the god Brahma the creator of the of the new Universe.

Illustration 6.1: Granite sculpture of Supreme God Vishnu, Dashavatara temple, 6th century CE, Deogarh, Madhya Pradesh, India

The Greatest Deity

Historically, Vedic sages treated Vishnu as a minor deity in the beginning but the accretion of Avatars and other celestial events related to Pole star transformed Him to an ultimate God with universal powers to govern the Cosmos. Lord Vishnu was the first astronomer of the world. The Vedic demigods never practiced any religion other than worshipping the nature itself. Not until they encountered with a unique problem of Vega, which used to be the pole star, fell down below the horizon due to the "Precession of the Equinoxes", they didn't realize the importance of Lord Vishnu and his contributions to the Astronomy.

The Ancient Indians believed that the same cosmic powers that create and destroy the Universe should also be the maintainer and preserver of the Pruthvi and Nakshatras, hence Vishnu has become central focus for the vast number of devotees during the puranic era. In the past, several religious cults were in existence in ancient India. The people who consider Vishnu as the supreme deity were combined under the common umbrella called as "Vaishnavism"; people who practice Vaishnavism today are called as Vaishnavites.

The concept of Vaishnavism at the meta-physical level is far more interesting than any other sci-fi fiction available to date. Let us say if you are the person who believes in the concept of Virtual reality or if you think that the whole Universe is a software program. Then the Lord Bramha becomes the global administrator from another dimension and Lord Vishnu will be the universal programmer from the infinite dimension. Lord Vishnu enters each and every Universe through his Avatars (re-incarnations). The Vedic Sages worshipped the super natural powers and they didn't develop the concept of worshipping a single God not until 8,000 BCE. Around 6,000 BCE, the Sages came up with an idea of Universal soul and re-birth based on the Karma. Lord Krishna's Karma Siddhanta was based on the concept that the journey of life doesn't end with the death of a body, it goes beyond that based on the Gunas (load of characters). The Soul carries the Gunas in a subtle form in its journey from one life to another. Even if you combine Theory of relativity and Quantum mechanics, it's not possible to model this hypothetical concept of Soul. It's relatively easy to come up with a fantasy theory like Virtual Universe, Parallel Universe, Projected Universe, Matrix-202, a Universe in a Computer simulation, holographic Universe etc., but it's very tough to come up with a mathematical model to prove the idea of Soul.

Around 1100 CE, the Southern Indian Vaishnava philosopher known as '**Ramanuja**' was a force behind the '**Shri Vaishnava**' movement. This movement was based on the amalgamation of several groups such as the religious cult that practiced Pancharata ritual and theology, the Tamil Alvars (Vaishnava poets of Southern India) and the people who practiced Orthodox Vedanta. **Ramanuja was critical of the Advaita Vedanta (Absolute monism of Sankara) in which an individual attains complete knowledge when he experiences the realization that the whole universe is Brahman (Being), this leads to a paradox, at which point the individuality itself is lost**[4]. More than 5000 years ago, to be exact on the first day of Mahabharata war (November 6, 3138 BCE), mythical city Dwaraka King, Lord Krishna delivered a sermon to the Pandavas warrior Arujuna who was reluctant to fight with his own cousins. During the 4th or 3rd century BCE, the conversation between Arjuna and Krishna which was originally in the verbal form (around 700 Sanskrit poems), written into a textual form and it's now called as "Bhagvad-Gita".

India's father of the nation, Mohandas Karamchand Gandhi (1869 AD – 1948 AD), who almost single handedly kicked out British Empire from India, translated the Sanskrit version of Bhagvad Gita to English language to unite 400 Million Hindus for his "Satyagraha" (Non-

Violent) movement against British. It was a huge publicity to the Vaishnavism. Why did Gandhi try to bring Bhakti into his political movement? He probably found some common ground between his belief in Satya (Truth) and the teachings of the Lord Krishna (An incarnation of Supreme God Vishnu) on Karma-yoga. Most recently, ISKCON (International Society for Krishna Consciousness) was responsible for worldwide distribution of Gaudiya Vaishnavism. As per the 'Encyclopedia Britannica', approximately 560 million people around the world practice Vaishnavism.

Dasakritikrite

Jayadeva a Sanskrit poet of 1200 CE was instrumental in popularizing Dashavatara, the ten incarnations of the supreme God Vishnu in another form called 'Dasakritikrite'. The Gita Govinda (song of Govinda) is a work composed by Jayadeva, it describes the relationship between Krishna and the gopikas (female cow herders) of Vrindhavan, and about the Krishna's sweetheart, Gopika named "Radha". The Gita Govinda is organized into Twelve chapters and each chapter divided into 24 sub-divisions called Prabhandhas. The text elaborates the "Ashta Nayika", eight moods of a heroine, this has been inspiration for many compositions and choreographic works in the classical dances such as Odyssey and other Southern Indian dances. The department of Posts (India) released a set of commemorative stamps and first day covers as a depiction and celebration of Jayadeva's Sanskrit composition on Dashavatara (Illustration 6.2).

Dashavatara (Ten Avatars)

There are some regional variations on how the ten avatars of Vishnu evolved, but the following list is most widely accepted in various traditions.

1. Matsya (Kruta yuga)

Illustration 6.2: Odisha poet Jayadeva's Geetagovinda (a Dashavatara in a different format called as '**Dasakritikrite**'), 1200 CE
(Photo Credit: Indian postal department)

2. Kurma (Kruta yuga)
3. Varaha (Kruta yuga)
4. Narasimha (Kruta yuga)
5. Vamana (Treta yuga)
6. Parushurama (Treta yuga)

7. Rama (Treta yuga)
8. Krishna (Dwapara yuga)
9. Buddha (Kali yuga)
10. Kalki (the incarnation yet to come)

The first four avatars took place in the Kruta yuga (some people call it as Satya yuga), the next three occurred in the Treta yuga, and the 8th and 9th in the Dwapara and Kali yuga respectively. There is an evolution theory exists for the first four avatars, the life originated in the sea and Matsya (fish) is the first Vertebrate, Kurma (tortoise) being an amphibian could survive both on land and sea, Narasimha represents the next big step in evolution of Homo sapiens.

Matsya Avatar

The meaning of Matsya in Sanskrit is a Fish. As per the mythology Vishnu takes this form in Kruta yuga to save Manavas (humans) from the deluge (great flood), the Vedic sages dedicated this avatar to the development of the boat and that is how the river and sea trading began in ancient India. But there is an another evolution theory which predicts that the life started in water as a fish and gradually developed into various other complex forms over the period of time and finally ended up as humans.

Kurma Avatar

This was the second avatar that presumably occurred during the Kruta yuga. As per the legend, Vishnu took the tortoise form to bear the weight of the mount Mandara when the Devas and the Asuras decided to churn the Ocean of milk to get Amrita, the beverage of immortality (Illustration 6.3). The churning went on for more than thousand years. But, at the end, the Devas ditched the Asuras and gave them wine and spared Amrita for themselves, which they thought vital for their survival and supremacy over the Asuras.

The demons realized the injustice and demanded Amrita. Lord Vishnu assumes the form of Mohini (beautiful woman) and agrees to distribute it equally. Mohini requests the Devas and Asuras to form two separate lines. The asuras were drunk and totally mesmerized by the beauty of Mohini and hardly able to notice Mohini's partial attitude towards Devas. One cleaver asura named Rahu joined Devas line in the form of the Chandra (Moon) and drank some Amrita. Vishnu noticed this and cut off the head of Rahu with his Sudharshana chakra. But it was too late, Rahu already drank amrita and attained immortality. Rahu prayed the Lord Vishnu for a boon so that he can swallow Sun and Moon occasionally. A mythology that describes the concept behind the solar and lunar eclipses.

Kurma avatar tells us the way in which Vedic sages discovered the phenomenon of Solar and Lunar eclipses and how they named the celestial objects after the gods. Interestingly, none of the asuras were part of the Vedic astronomy except Rahu and Kethu. But this is not the end of this Avatar, there are a lot more things to explore, let us take a look at the complete symbolism of the Samudra Manthan. As mentioned in the Vishnu Purana the Devas' king Indra lost his kingdom because he was cursed by the powerful Sage Durvasa; Indra went to the Lord Vishnu for the help.

Q. Pretty much every avatar of Supreme God Vishnu begins with Indra losing his Swargaloka and turning to the Lord Vishnu for the help, what does it mean by Indra lost his Kingdom?

A. There is no special meaning here other than the fact that this episode was initiated by the Sage **Durvasa** who wanted the Himalayan Sages to brain storm with Dravidian Siddhas who possess an advanced knowledge in Astronomy, Ayurveda, Agriculture and other fields.

Q. The Puranas also mentioned that the Lord Vishnu suggested Indra to form an alliance with Asuras (Dravidians in this case) and churn the Palasamundar (Ocean of Milk) to get Amrutha (nectar of immortality). The great snake and semi-god 'Vasuki' agreed to remain as the churning rope and the Mount Mandara as the churning rod based on the request from the Deva guru Brihaspati. What is the true symbolism of Samudra Manthan and where is mount Mandara located?

A. As per the legend the Sage Brihaspati, the priest of the Devas, was instrumental in alliance between Asuras and Devas. They agreed to team up and eventually met on the top of the mount Mandara. Based on the historical accounts of the Greek traveler Megasthenes (**300 BCE**), the Mallus mountain lies to the north-west of ancient Tamralipti (modern name Tamulk), a renowned sea-port of that era. The historians now identify the Mallus mountain with the Parshvanath hills of south Bihar, the puranic name of which was Mandara mountain (Illustration 6.4).

The process of Ocean churning began with Asuras holding the head of Vasuki and the Devas the tail on the right-hand side of the mount Mandara. Within a short span of time they met with various challenges, the Mandara mountain began to sink, fortunately Lord Vishnu came to rescue it from sinking in the form of Kurma avatar (Turtle – the second incarnation).

Lord Shiva swallows Halahalam: The first byproduct of the churning of the milk of ocean was Halahalam (lethal poison); based on the advice from Lord Vishnu, the Asuras and Suras (devas) approached the Lord Shiva and requested him to save the world. The Bola Shankar (another name for Shiva, who can be easily persuaded) swallows the lethal poison, but his wife Parvathi prevents the poison descending into his body. The color of Shiva's neck turns blue because the poison remains trapped at the neck and Shiva earns the title 'Neela Kanteshwara'.

Illustration 6.3: Samudra Mathanam: The churning of the Ocean of Milk, Asuras on the left and the Suras on the right (acknowledged to bazaar art print, c.1910's)

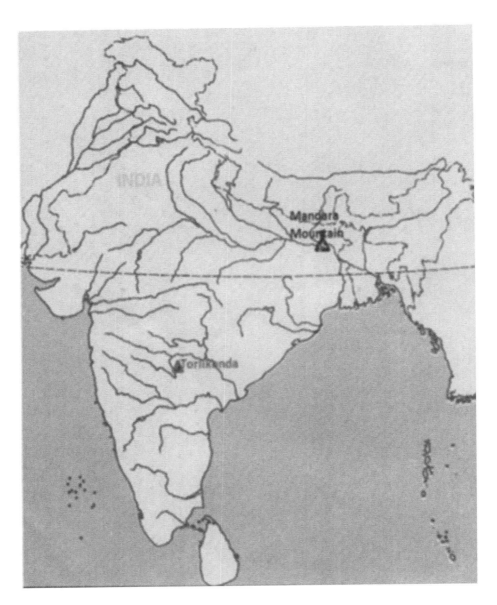

Illustration 6.4: Mount Mandara, present day Parshvanath hills of South Bihar, India (Not to scale)

Symbolism: The Samudra Manthan session between Asuras and Devas begins with the Sages explaining the importance 5th Chakra of Human body, Neela Chakra (Blue color) [1] as shown in the Illustration 6.5. The Blue chakra represents the neck and communication skills, which indirectly refer to Lord Shiva's Neela Kanta. As the result of the churning, fourteen magnificent treasures emerged from the ocean as shown in the table 6.1. Let us summarize the accomplishments of the Samudra Manthan based on the Vedic symbolism:

1) Lord Vishnu and Goddess Laxmi represent the south celestial pole and north celestial poles of Vedic Astronomy respectively
2) The objects emerged represent the twelve constellations of the Vedic Astrology

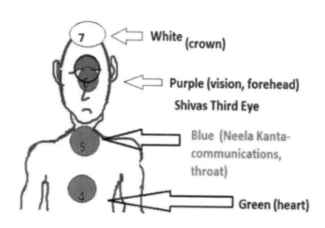

Illustration 6.5:   Chakra System of human body based on color coding

The Ayurvedic physician Dhanvantri represents the transfer of Ayurvedic knowledge from Asuras to Devas. The Dravidians were frequently referred to as Asuras, who were the original inventors of Ayurveda (ancient medicine) and shared the knowledge with their North Indian counterparts. The authors of Dashavatara noted that the knowledge transfer was one sided, the Asuras didn't gain much out of it. This is evident from the story of Rahu and Keta and the way Mohini (Lord Vishnu) distributed the Amrita. The Kurma avatar probably represents the first ever summit of Dravidian Shiddas from Southern India and the Vedic Sages from North India.

Table 6.1: List of Treasures uncovered during the Samudra Manthan

Treasure Type	Treasure emerged from the Ocean	God/Asura who got the treasure
Goddess of Wealth	Lakshmi	God Vishnu
Apsaras	Heavenly Nymphs (Ramba, Urvashi, Thilothama)	Indra
Sura Goddess	Varuni	Asuras
Wish-fulfilling Tree	Kalpavriksha	All
Wish-fulfilling cow	Kamdhenu	Sages
Wish-fulfilling gem	Chintamani	Lord Vishnu
Seven-headed flying horse	Ucchaishaba	Asuras
Elephant	Airavata	Indra
Conch	Panchajanya	Devas
Bow	Saranga	Asuras
Moon	Chandra	Devas
Ayurveda Physician	Dhanvantari	Devas
Elixir of Immortality	Amrita	Devas and Rahu Ketu; Lord Vishnu in the form of enchantress Mohini bewitched the demons.

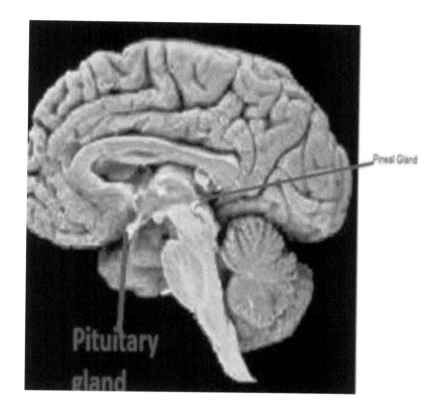

Illustration 6.6: The Cross section of human Brain showing the locations of the Pineal and Pituitary glands

Q. What is Amrita (**Elixir of Immortality**) made of?

A. Amrita, **an elixir of immortality** is a state of intoxication caused by the consumption of Soma juice. Soma is a juice extracted from the fermented Vippa flowers and mixed with Bhāng. The Bhāng is a mild marijuana made from young leaves of Indian Hemp plant. The consumption of Bhāng is allowed in India for adults on certain festivals such as Holi, a Hindu spring festival played with colors. The consumption of Soma juice almost certainly activates the sixth chakra

'Ajña'.   The physical activity, which is the tug of war (Samudra Manthan) activates the 7th chakra 'Sahasrara'. The nectar produced by the Sahasrara and received by the Ajña is called as 'Amrita'.

According to Jane Dixon (author of The Biology of Kundalini) and Cyndi Dale (Author of Llewellyn's Complete Book of Chakras), the Amrita is combination of chemicals[2], neurotransmitters, hormones, and amino acids such as Vasopressin - a hormone that controls the water retention; Endogenous Cannabinoids – that affects appetite, mood, pain, inflammatory response and memory; Ca2+ - Calcium ions helps with passing information between neurons and regulates the cell function; Oxytocin – relieves the pain and induces self-esteem and optimism, and Polarized water which improves the intermolecular network generated from the Glial cells and neurons. Based on the research topic published in science direct[4], there is an evidence that the glial cells play an important role in modulating neurotransmission, control information flow between neurons and development and recovery of synapses.

As per the latest research, the activation of the Ajña chakra, either slows down the body growth (a step towards immortality) or increases it based on the body types. The ancient Sages probably aware of this kundalini effect and hence referred to this as the drink of immortality. When Ajña chakra is activated it involves the Pineal gland which is in the middle of the brain, also called as "Thrinetra" or Shiva's third eye.

The Pineal gland produces the hormone called Melatonin, the same neurotransmitter which helps bears hibernate[3]. The Melatonin helps to control the human body's biological cycle, it regulates the sleep and wake up cycles, lowers the heart rate so that you can live longer, increases the immune function, and blocks the anti-depression and SAD (seasonal affective disorder) by boosting the Serotonin levels in the brain.

Per the article 'Shiva-yoga and Pineal Gland' which is taken from H.H. Mahatapasvi Shri Kumarswamiji's book, – '**Technique of Opening the Third Eye'.**

"The pineal gland is an oval shaped body about the size of a pea lying in the middle of the head, behind and just above the pituitary. It contains pigment like that found in the eyes and is connected by two nerve cords with the optic thalamus. Since it controls the action of the light upon the body scientists have suggested that it is a remnant of the third eye. The third eye is an enigmatic organ having a universal history. It is the middle eye of Shiva, …The third eye is an organ apparently dormant but innately acquired by mankind, whose awakening is the right of every individual. It is an organ of inner vision which embraces eternity while our physical eyes look before us seeing neither past nor future. He who has opened this third eye can direct and control the energies of matter, see all things in the eternal now and so be in touch with causes, reveal the etheric records and see clairvoyantly. It is through medium of the third eye that an Adept can at any moment put himself in touch with his disciple anywhere."

Varaha Avatar

As per the myth, Vishnu in Varaha (wild boar) form saves the earth from the clutches of the asura Hiranyaksha, who submerged it to the bottom of cosmic ocean. The Varaha grew to enormous size and then dove into the depths of the cosmic ocean and brought the earth back to the surface. Not exactly sure, what was the intention of the Vedic Sages in creating this avatar. Did they mean the Varaha played a role in saving the earth from ice age caused due to the galactic rotation or did it play a role in saving it from the solar flares? According to some people, this avatar represents the wild animal, the boar moving from water to land, a next big step in the evolution. The DNA of boar matches 99% with humans, that's why eating a pig is considered as cannibalism by majority of population in India.

Narasimha Avatar

As per the legend, Lord Vishnu assumes the half-man and half-lion form to save the world from the atrocities of the Rakshasa (Demon) Hiranyakashpa. Lord Vishnu manifested himself as man-lion from a stone pillar in the twilight zone (Sandhya Samayam, neither day nor night, it's the time when the birds return to nests), and took Hiranyakashpa upon his lap and killed him. This avatar was needed because Hiranyakashpa obtained a boon from Lord Shiva so that he could be killed neither by a man nor by the God; neither during the day time nor during the night; and neither on earth nor in the heaven. Narasimha could kill Hiranyakashpa because he was neither God nor man (the half-man and half-animal form). Lord Narasimha is one of the most powerful deities and worshipped by many people even today in several parts of Telangana (south central India), South India, Orissa and East India.

This incident might have occurred around 11,000 BCE, when there was a large influx of Indo-European races into South India and Deccan. Based on the Tamil records, the heads of Velan and Suran races wore Ox and Horse Skull as the protective gear for the head during the fights. The Mahishasura was the Velan leader. There might be some other unidentified race or Aryan tribe which wore the skull of Lion as the helmet and that tribal leader might have killed the Asura King Hiranyakashpa.

Vamana Avatar

 The fifth incarnation of the Supreme God Vishnu, utilizes Vamana (a dwarf) as the "device of deceit" to defeat the mighty asura Mahabali (Bali Chakravarty). This is the only avatar in which asura Bali was on the path of righteousness whereas the Devas were on the wrong side. This avatar raises the serious question of what is the righteous path? The people of Kerala were deeply moved by the treachery of Devas, that's why they celebrate Onam. As per the myth, Lord Vishnu allowed Mahabali to return to his kingdom once a year. Every year in the Malayalam month of Chingam (either August or September), the people of Kerala celebrate this festival as homecoming event of the mythical king Mahabali.

Parasurama Avatar

The Sixth incarnation of Vishnu, a killer of his own mother in the name of Peethru dharma, went on a violent rampage to kill all the Kshatriya kings who didn't follow Vedic dharma. How dumb on part of the barbaric Sages of Mount Meru to attribute an avatar to a mass murderer? They probably applied the same old rule, everything is fair in war. Parasurama was an expert in archery and did many tapasyas to get Divya-Astras from Shiva and other Sages and Gods. Not a single king or their army was able to stand in front of Parasurama's archery power combined with Divya-Astras. He slaughtered many kings and established Brahmin rule everywhere, that was time when other castes such as Vysyas or Brahmins entered the ruling class. The Vedic Sages were either happy or scared of Parasurama and finally awarded him with Vishnu incarnation for his achievements in establishing the Vedic dharma everywhere.

Sri Rama - 7th incarnation

Rama was the least powerful god of all the incarnations. Rama never had any super natural powers, but he was recognized and known by various Sages such as Vishwamitra and Agastya since his childhood. As a thirteen-old boy, he exhibited heroic efforts in saving the Yagnas from the Rakshasa attacks. In the name of Sanatana Dharma, he led the Vanara army and built the bridge on the sea to kill the most powerful Daithya king of Treta yuga, Ravana. Rama went above and beyond known Dharmas of that time, the sages had no option but to grant him the 7th incarnation of Supreme God Vishnu.

Sri Krishna

Self-proclaimed eighth incarnation of Lord Vishnu, the king of mythical city Dwaraka, original author of the most famous Karma Siddhanta book of Hindus, "Bhagvad Gita". The literal meaning of Krishna is Samana (sort of blueish dark complexion) color. The sermon, Lord Krishna gave to Arjuna on the battlefield of Kurukshetra was later compiled by Sage Veda Vyas known as the 'Bhagvad Gita". When Arjuna was reluctant and not willing to fight against his own cousins, family members and friends, Lord Krishna reminded Arjuna about his Kshatriya Dharma (caste bound duty) and manifested himself as the Supreme God through application of Māyā yoga.

These teachings by Lord Krishna about the various routes to liberation to Arjuna in the form of "song of the Lord" called as 'Bhagvad-Gita'. Krishna was the main "Sutradhari" (meaning architect) of Maha Bharata war, as the charioteer of Arjuna, he influenced each and every bit of the war. Lord Krishna influenced the great Himalayan sages of Dwapara yuga, Vyasa and Narada with his teachings on Karma Yoga and Māyā Yoga, they had no option but to treat him as the incarnation of the supreme God Vishnu.

There were some hymns dedicated to Indra in Vedas but people won't worship Indra as a god, because Lord Krishna advised the villagers and citizens of Aryavarta against praying Indra. Lord Krishna saved the villagers from the   angry rain god Indra by lifting the mount Govardhana, another act of Māyā as shown in the Illustration 6.7. There will be an obvious question, what is Māyā? The Mahabharata and Puranic texts talk about at least half a dozen Māyā incidents of Lord

Krishna. What exactly is Māyā? Is it an illusion or a black magic trick done by the Lord Krishna?

Illustration 6.7: Sri Krishna lifting the mount Govardhana to rescue Yadavas from the aggression of Devas' king Indra (6th - 7th century granite sculpture, Ellora caves; ©ASI)

As per the A. K. Coomaraswamy, a legendary Tamil philosopher of 20th Century, the definition of Māyā is as given below:

"He who produces manifestation by means of his 'art' is the Divine Architect, and the world is his 'art'; as such the world is neither more nor less unreal than are our own works of art, which, because of their relative impermanence, are also unreal if compared to the art that 'resides' in the artist."

So, its preferable to translate 'Māyā' as an 'art' rather than 'illusion', as noted by the author René Guénon[5] in his book 'Studies in Hinduism'.

Buddha - 9th incarnation

The Shrimad Bhagavata doesn't consider Buddha as the 9th incarnation of Supreme God Vishnu, for obvious reasons most of the people aware of, Buddha didn't accept the Vedic authority.   In spite of this many Hindus treat Siddhartha Gautama as the incarnation of Lord Vishnu. A majority of Buddhist teachings derived from Vedic scriptures. But, one of the most appealing factors of Buddhism was Buddha's teachings about putting an end to the animal ritual sacrifice. The bloody Kalinga war transformed the Emperor Ashoka into a Buddhist monk. He sent orders to end "Animal sacrifice". This forced the later generations to accept Buddha as the God. The four famous trees describe the complete history of the Shakyamuni (Sage of Sakyas, another name for Buddha). The first tree in Lumbini Park (bordering India and Nepal), where he was born under a tree. The second one is the Bodhi tree at Bodhi Gaya where Buddha attained enlightenment (became Buddha) beneath this Bodhi tree. The third one is in the deer park, Sarnath under this tree he proclaimed "Dhamma" (his first Sermon). Finally, he attained Mahaparinirvana (final decease) under the Sal-tree at Kusinagara.

Buddha converted thousands of people of Magadha to his spiritual tribe.   His followers include King Bimbisara and his 32 queens. Buddha's apostles include   royal officers, noblemen, bankers, traders, daivajnas and even thousands of Brahmins. It was a point of time in the history when there was a conflict between Tyrant Vedic Brahmins and the ruling class (Kshatriyas). That is when the Buddha showed them an alternate path.   The Buddhism vanished out of India more than thousand years ago, because of the factors such as negative doctrines, over emphasis on monastic life and absence of any object of worship etc.

7. Lord Shiva

"The pure soul, cleansed through the control of breadth and meditation soon attains salvation. And becomes one with God through yogic Samadhi"

(Atharva Veda 6.51.1)

Chronology

7400 BCE – 7300 BCE Lord Shiva along with 12 Siddhas crosses Vindhyas and settles at mount Kailash

7000 BCE – 4000 BCE Revelation of Vedas and Agamas; Vedic Sarasvatī-Indus civilization; invention of Yoga & Meditation by Vedic Sages on the banks of the lost river Vedic Sarasvatī; it was a combined effort of the Sages who migrated from Deccan as well as the Himalayan Sages.

4000 BCE – 3000 BCE Construction of First **Somnath** Temple at Sauraushtra, the Triveni Sangam of three rivers Kapila, Hiran and mythical river Saraswathi, as per the Hindu legend, the temple was built with Gold.

1500 BCE Advaita Vedanta (Adi Shankara's Hindu Philosophy) introduces Yoga for the first time. Construction of modern Shiva temple at Kedarnath, North India.

300 BCE – 300 CE Construction of Lord Siva temple at Srikalahasti, (the first south Indian Shiva Temple) by various Kings of **Trilingadesa** (original Telangana before Andhra was sold to Madras). The Temple complex was renovated by various Kings of Cholas, Pallavas and Pandian dynasties between 3rd century CE and 16th century CE.

400 BCE - 200 BCE Sage Patanjali introduces "Yoga sutras of Patanjali" – a compilation of 196 Yoga sutras, mostly extracted from the old Yogic traditions.

480 CE – 767 CE Vallabhi Kings re-build Somanath temple

650 CE – 800 CE Early Tantras were composed

700 CE – 728 CE Pallavas built Shore Temple at Mahabalipuram

765 CE – 733 CE   Raja Krishna-I constructs Khailasa temple to Shiva at Ellora

900 CE – 1150 CE   The Chandelas built majestic Mahadeva Temple at Khajuraho

1238 CE – 1255 CE   Utkal King Narasimhadeva-I built the magnificent Temple of Konark

1173 CE – 1213 CE   Kakatiyas built Ramappa Temple at Palampet village near Warangal, Telangana, India

1780 CE   The most famous Shiva temple, Shri Kashi Viswanath temple rebuilt by the Maratha ruler, Maharani Ahilya Bai Holkar.

Lord Shiva an epithet of Rudra

Unlike other deities, **Lord Shiva** was dubbed as the "**destroyer**", because the Sages needed to complement the supreme God Vishnu as the "preserver" and Lord Brahma as the "creator" to balance the Hindu Trinity. Lord Shiva is known by various names, the Tantric called him Bhairava (Frightful). The Tamils call him the Lord Nataraja; meaning 'the Comic dancer'. The North Indians called him Mahadeva (Great God) and the Vedic seers call him Rudra (roarer). During the Vedic period, Rudra was probably more closely associated with Asuras rather than the Devas. Because Rudra's name was mentioned few times in the Vedas. Rudra was also treated as an outsider by the Gods and Sages of Mount Meru Vedic gang.

Something has changed during the Sandhya Samayam (a transition period from Treta Yuga to Dwapara Yuga), Rudra lost his epithet, and Shiva became the main deity for the non-brahmins. Although, the Lord Shiva was designated as the destroyer by his adversaries, his Non-Brahmin Shaiva devotees always considered Him as the total power over the Cosmos. There is an ancient saying in Telugu "**Shivude Aagna Lenedhe, Chimaina Kuttadhu**"; meaning no action takes place in the Universe, not even an ant bite, without Lord Shiva's permission. This shows that the ancient people probably knew on a philosophical or meta-physical level that Lord Shiva is the only God in the entire Universe. And the Shiva-Linga represents the symbol of Consciousness at the Cosmic level.

Blasphemy on the hierophany of Jyothilinga

The Ajitagama clearly describes Shiva Linga as a pillar of life, so any other interpretation of Jyothilinga must be rejected. Many Shaivites commented on the web:

"It's totally absurd some of the 19th century translators of Shivaism seem to have an imaginary invention on the image of Shiva Lingam as a 'phallic symbol'. Since Lord Shiva described as no form, it's ridiculous to compare Shiva with a human figure."

According to Swami Vivekananda (Paris, 1900) "the Shiva-Linga had its origin in the idea of the Yupa-Stambha or Skambha, the sacrificial post, idealized in Vedic rituals as the symbol of Eternal Brahman". Shaivism is the only culture that is equally popular amongst both Urban as well as tribal populations for the last 6000 years.

Agamas

Agamas (meaning - traditions) are the Non-Vedic collection of Sanskrit scriptures, there were no authors, presumably revered by the Lord Shiva just like Lord Brahma revered the Vedas. Until the 11th century CE the Vedas and Agamas were treated under the same category "Sruti" (it means no authors), after which period the Sanskrit Nighantu named Vedas as the '**Nigamas**' and the Tantras as the '**Agamas**'. The Agamas also sometimes called as Tantras, there are three main divisions, the Shaiva Agamas, Vaishnava Agamas and the Shakta-Agamas. The Shaivism based on Shaiva Agamas revere the Ultimate Reality as the Lord Shiva, similarly the Vaishnava Agamas (such as Vaikahanasas Samhitas and Pancharata) and Shakti-Agamas (Tantras) adore ultimate reality as Vishnu and Shakti respectively. Based on the excavations by Archeological Survey of India, the Tantric origins (proto-Shiva) can be traced back to the Indus valley Vedic Culture as far as 4000 BCE.

Shaiva Agamas

The modern Tamil Shaiva Siddhanta originated in the 10th century CE from the devotional compositions of the 'Nayamars', which was based on the Twenty-eight Shaiva Agamas, Nigamas (Vedas) and the hymns of other Tamil literary sources such as Tirumurai.

Shaiva Agamas				
S. No	Name	Number of Slokhas	Revealed by the face of Shiva	Name of the Rishi who owned the Agamas
1	Kamikagama	Parartha	Sadyojata	Kaushika
2	Yogaja	Laksha	Sadyojata	Kaushika
3	Chintya	Laksha	Sadyojata	Kaushika
4	Karana	Koti	Sadyojata	Kaushika
5	Ajitagama	Laksha	Sadyojata	Kaushika
6	Dipta	Laksha	Vamadeva	Kasyapa
7	Sukshma	Padma	Vamadeva	Kasyapa
8	Sahasraka	sangama	Vamadeva	Kasyapa
9	Amshumat	Five Lakhs	Vamadeva	Kasyapa
10	Suprabhedagama	Three Crores	Vamadeva	Kasyapa
11	Vijaya	Three Crores	Aghora	Bharadvaja
12	Nihshvasa	One Crore	Aghora	Bharadvaja
13	Svayambhuva	One and half Crore	Aghora	Bharadvaja
14	Anala (Agneya)	Thirty thousand	Aghora	Bharadvaja

15	Vira	Lakh	Aghora	Bharadvaja
16	Raurava	Ten crore	Tatpurusha	Gautama
17	Makutagama	Lakh	Tatpurusha	Gautama
18	Vimala	Three Lakhs	Tatpurusha	Gautama
19	Chandrajnana	Three crore	Tatpurusha	Gautama
20	Mukhabimba	Lakh	Tatpurusha	Gautama
21	Prodgita	Three Lakhs	Isana	Agastya
22	Lalita	Eight Lakhs	Isana	Agastya
23	Siddha	Two lakhs	Isana	Agastya
24	Santana	Twelve lakhs	Isana	Agastya
25	Sarvokta	Six Lakhs	Isana	Agastya
26	Parameshvara	Two lakhs	Isana	Agastya
27	Kirana	Five crores	Isana	Agastya
28	Vatula	Lakh	Isana	Agastya

Table 7.1: The Shaiva Agamas

Lakh   1,00,000; Crore 10,000,00;
Paartta 100, 000, 000, 000, 000, 000;
Padma   1, 000, 000, 000, 000, 000
Sangama 100, 000, 000, 000, 000

Agamas the Fifth Veda?

There is always a strong argument on whether the Agama should be considered as 5th Veda or Cosmic Veda.

As per Suprabhed Agama:

"The Siddhanta(agama) consists of the essence of the Veda". Mukuta Agama mentions "This tantra(agama) is of the essence of the Veda. This Siddhanta (agama) knowledge which is the significance of Vedanta is supremely good".

Per Swami Prajnanananda, quoted by Sir John Woodroffe:

" .. the Agamic (tantric) texts, as we known them today, had for the most part preceded Buddhism, and only the Agamic cult had been able gradually to swallow up Buddhism on the Indian sub-continent, and ultimately to banish it altogether from the Indian soil; it was not the Upanishadic philosophy but the Agamic cult that was responsible for the supplanting of Buddhism and for the fusion of its salient features into the core of the Hindu religion..."

Per M. Gnanapiragasam, Former Principal, Parameswara College, Jaffna, Sri Lanka:

"… The Pidagagama is the name given to the Buddhist Scripture Tripidaga. This came into existence immediately after the Buddha attained Nirvana. The nomenclature of the Buddhist religious treatise was obviously taken from the then existing Saiva treatises. Hence we may conclude that the Saiva Agamas were in existence before the 6th century BCE..."

S. No	Chakra	Associated body part	Color scheme
1	Muladhara	Root (Base of Spine)	Red
2	Svadhistana	Sacral	Orange
3	Manipura	Solar Plexus	Yellow
4	Anahata	Heart	Green
5	Visuddha	Throat	Blue
6	Ajna	Forehead (Pituitary Gland)	Purple
7	Shasrara	Crown	White

Table 7.2: List of Chakras

Chakras

The human body consists of seven energy points called as Chakras as shown in the Table 7.2. Through Yoga, the Tantric attains bliss of liberation (Pure-consciousness) by awakening the Kundalini (the serpent power) lying dormant at the root-center (Muladhara Chakra), and it flows up through successive focal points until it reaches the highest point called as SAHASRARA Chakra (also called as Sahasrara Padma). Each Chakra is associated with the underlying body part. For example, the pituitary gland represents the Ajna Chakra (Shiva's third eye) whereas the throat (Shiva's Blue throat) represents the Visuddha chakra.

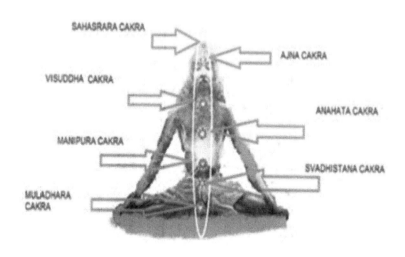

Illustration 7.1: The chakras located in the human body

How to Transcend Death?

Professor Eknath Easwaran of Nagpur University wrote the following in his book '**God Makes the Rivers to flow**':

"**Lord Shiva** is represented traditionally as the Divine Beggar, who comes with his begging bowl to your door for alms. When you offer this beggar the food, clothes, money, he refutes to accept them.

"What do you want from me then?" you ask.

"Your **ego**," comes the answer.

"Your **selfishness**, your **separateness**. Throw that in my bowl and become united with Mrityunjaya, Conqueror of Death."

The conclusion here, the yoga and meditation along with proper diet might help you attain pure-consciousness. To Transcend death, one should also give up false ego, selfishness, arrogance and don't get parted from mass population. The latest example is Mahatma Gandhi, his physical body left the world but his ideas on non-violence still alive in the minds of Millions of people.

8. Mahishasura Mardini

"Recognition of the world as the manifestation of Śakti is worship of Śakti. Pure knowledge, unrelated to objects, is absolute."

-Devīkālottara Āgama

Chronology

5500 BCE – 5000 BCE[1]

The epic battle between the woman warrior **Chamundeshwari** (Goddess Durga or Umai) and Asura **Mahishasura,** which lasted for 9 days in the suburbs of Srirangapatnam, Karnataka, India. The place is now called as Chamundi Hills of Mysore city.

245 BCE – 250 BCE

The Third Buddhist convocation held at Pataliputra, the Buddhist records referred to this place Mysore as the Mahisha Mandala.

6th century CE – 7th Century CE

Era of Reconnaissance of Mahishasuramardini (Durga Slaying Mahishasura) in south India. The sculptures of Goddess Durga showed up in the Mahabalipuram and Ellora caves.

1799 CE

The British killed the Muslim ruler of Srirangapatnam Tipu Sultan and handed over the city and the surrounding towns including the Chamundi Hills to the local Maharajas which they named as **Mysore** to commemorate the killing of the Demon Mahishasura.

Who is Mahishasura?

As per the Hindu Mythology, Rambha (not the heavenly nymph from the courts of Indra), the Asura King fell in love with a she-buffalo and eventually led to the nuptial canopy. This story is quite fascinating, the therianthropic child, partly human with buffalo head, born to this unusual couple was named Mahishasura. The etymology of the word Mahishasura (buffalo demon King), derived from the fact that Mahisha means Buffalo or water buffalo and Asura means antigod or demon. As per the legend, Mahishasura went to forest and performed Tapasyas until Brahma appears and gives him a boon. When the Lord Brahma appeared, the Mahishasura asked for immortality so that he could defeat the Devas.

God Brahma was helpless because everything that was born should ultimately die and asked him to pick something else instead. Then Mahishasura choose a boon in such a way neither Gods nor Men could kill him, and he either forgot or underestimated the power of women. With the new-found power Mahishasura started war with Devas and defeated them, that's where Goddess Durga comes into picture and kills him because she was neither God nor a Man.

The Real Story

The Mahishasura was the head of the Velan tribe, an Indo-European race that migrated from deep south around 5500 BCE. The Velans used the Buffalo masks to protect themselves from the enemy attacks. The epic battle between woman warrior Chamundi and the buffalo man (the Velan tribe head with Buffalo mask) took place for nine days. Every time she destroyed the buffalo mask, the buffalo man used another mask until all the masks were destroyed and finally dead in the hands of Chamundi. That time onwards the woman worrier Chamundi became the goddess Mahishasuramardini.

Illustration 8.1: Goddess Durga slaying the demon Mahishasura
(7th century CE granite sculptor, south India ©ASI)

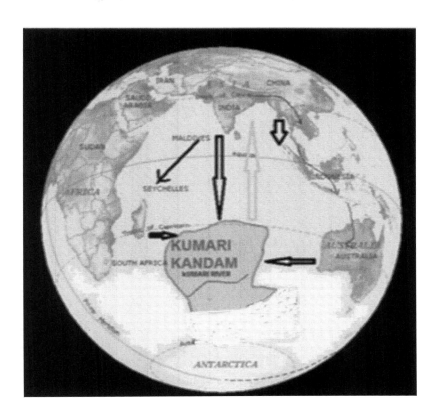

Illustration 8.2: Artistic view of lost continent Kumari Kandam in the Southern Indian Ocean

Where did the buffalo Men come from?

As per the author of the book 'The Origin of the Indo-European Races and Peoples", V. Chockalingam Pillai, these people migrated from the cradle, the Gondwana continent or Kumari Kandam (Illustration 10.2) that submerged into the south west Indian ocean. There is no archeological evidence found so far to confirm the existence of such continent. In fact, it may not be possible to find any such evidence because that area is surrounded by the active underground volcanoes. The human involvement in underwater exploration is too dangerous because of the active volcanos in the vicinity, any future explorations to find out the lost Kumari Kandam must include marine robots.

9. Gautama Buddha

"The Perfect Buddha,
The foremost of all Teachers I salute;
He has proclaimed
The Principle of Universal Relativity"

-Nagarjuna

(Buddhist Philosopher Nagarjuna, in his book Madhyamakakarika,
The founder of 3rd century CE Madhyamika school of Mahayana
Buddhism, University of Nalanda)

Chronology (BCE – before Christ)

567 BCE   Birth of **Gautama Siddhartha**; born in the Lumbini park near Kapilavastu[1] (present day Nepal) **

538 BCE   Great Renunciation, Siddhartha renounces the family life, left his summer palace and went to Rajagriha, the capital city of Magadha (at that time), where he learned Yoga and Upanishads from Brahmins.

532 BCE   Siddhartha attains enlightenment (becomes Buddha) while sitting under the Bodhi Tree, Buddha Gaya (present day, State of Bihar, India).

533 BCE - 488 BCE   Buddha preached meditation and spirituality at Rajagriha (Kingdom of Magadha) and Sravasti; during the 45-year tenure, Buddha transforms thousands of people as his followers and some of them even converted as bhikkhus (male monks) and Bhikkunis (female monks).

487 BCE   Buddha attains "Mahaparinirvana". Based on the Cingalese records, Mahaparinirvana took place 218 years before the coronation of the Emperor Ashoka; the puranic records of Magadha shows the date of coronation of Ashoka as 269 BCE.

** Some historians use 566 BCE as the working hypothesis

Life of Siddhartha as a Prince

Gautama Siddhartha, a descendant of the solar Sakya King was born in the garden of Lumbini near Kapilavastu (present day Nepal, illustration 9.1), on the way to a hospital in a nearby Kingdom. His mother, Mahamaya, the Sakya queen of Kapilavastu died one week after giving birth to the future Buddha.

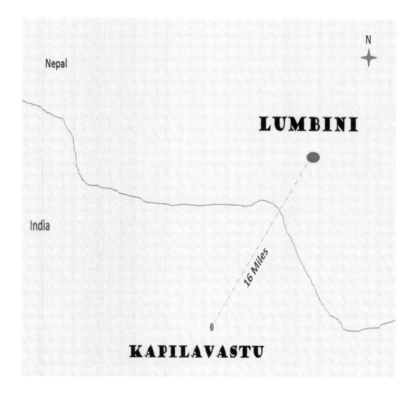

Illustration 9.1: Lumbini park (present day Nepal) near Kapilavastu
(Courtesy: Zircone Systems, Folsom, California)

Illustration 9.2: Lumbini Garden, birth of future Buddha
(reproduced from MAGADHA Architecture & Culture, 1942)

After analyzing the Janma Kundalini (birth stars) of Siddhartha, Astrologers predicted the new born would become either a monk or an Emperor (Chakravarty). Gautama Siddhartha's father always thought the first prediction might be possible. Because, the most powerful kingdoms such as Magadha were flourishing at that time. The odds of becoming an emperor were almost impossible. So, he decided to take every precaution to shield his son from the worldly worries. His father always wanted Sakyasimha to be the worrier, but he had shown early signs of meditation when he was a child.

Siddhartha's father King Suddhodana and the foster mother Mahapajapati Gotami completely isolated Buddha from the outside world and the miseries of Life. They appointed best teachers to educate him, the prince took part in athletics and learned how to use arms and horse riding in the company of his royal cousins and relatives. Siddhartha was good at athletics and studies and there was not a single reason why the King should be ashamed of his son other than worrying about the forecast made by the daivajnas, who warned that his son might become Buddha.

Yasodhara's Swayamvarum

King Suddhodana learned that his son likes the Yasodhara, a beautiful daughter of another royal family. So, he sent the messengers to Yasodhara's father to ask her hand in marriage with his son. But, as per the customs prevailing in those days, Yasodhara's father rejected the offer, instead asked Siddhartha to take part in the Swayamvarum, the tradition of Kshatriyas that a bride must be won in the open contest by feats of arrows, swords and horse racing. Everybody thought that Siddhartha is too gentle and hard to challenge other Kshatriyas and his royal cousins in the open contest. The main rival was Siddhartha's cousin Devadatta, who was good at Archery; there was another cousin Nanda, good at Sword fighting and Arjuna was expert at horse riding. All his royal cousins were in love with Yasodhara's beauty, so everybody showed up at the Swayamvarum. Surprisingly, Siddhartha did well in Archery much better than Devadatta; easily defeated Nanda in the Sword fighting and his famous white horse, Kantaka won the horse racing. The judges finally declared the Siddhartha as the winner and eligible to marry Yasodhara. King Suddhodana presented the newly married couple with a splendid palace, every care was taken to ensure that no hint of sadness or sorrow should distract their happiness. Siddhartha and Yasodhara had a son, whom they named Rahula.

Great Renunciation

The King Suddhodana still worried about the predictions of the astrologers, and he ordered the servants to never allow Siddhartha to go beyond the walls of the palace. But that didn't work out long time, Siddhartha soon realized that he should visit village and find out more about the outside world. One day he requested the King to allow him to visit the village and find out about the outside world. The King realized too much control over the married son might backfire, so he consented immediately, but told the villagers about his son's visit and instructed them not to allow any old or sick people on the streets.

Despite king's orders, while Siddhartha passing through the streets on his chariot, an old and sick man came out of his house to beg on the streets. Siddhartha saw the old and sick person for the first time in his entire life, out of profound amusement he asked Channa, the charioteer, about the person's appearance. The Channa said "This is an elderly sick person and everybody grows older over the time". The prince not satisfied with the Channa's answer asked again "do you mean all the men and women become like this?" Channa replied "yes". Siddhartha still not satisfied with the answer, asked Channa "Shell my father, too, Yasodhara and I, all become like this?". Channa replied again, "Yes, all men and women now living become like this – if they live so long". The prince kept quiet and didn't talk until they reached home.

Siddhartha decided to make a clandestine trip without informing his father. In the next visit, he took Channa and entered village not as prince, but in disguise, this time they bumped into another incident where a young person fell on the ground infected by the plague fever. "Channa, explain to me what is this?" Shidehara questioned. "This illness Sire, irrespective of age any one get this if they drink bad water or eat infected food, sometime it can spread from other infected persons too". Siddhartha realized there is so much suffering going on in the world and he needs to find out the answers for oldness and sickness. When they were walking towards the river bank, they saw a funeral procession where the dead body was carried out by a group of people. Siddhartha questioned again about the procession, "death Sire" Channa replied. This was the third greatest problem Siddhartha encountered so far. He asked Channa "will I, too, Yasodhara and my father, become like this one day?". "Yes, it's inevitable, after death people go to hell or heaven based on their deeds" visibly annoyed Channa replied immediately. Siddhartha didn't talk after that and returned to the Summer palace.

In the year 538 BCE (538 BC), at the age of 29, Siddhartha decided to leave the summer palace, his wife and son in search of finding the cure for "Old age, Sickness and Death". One full moon night he woke up and aroused Channa and ordered him to saddle Kantaka, his horse. He quietly walked out of the palace gates without looking at his sleeping wife and son; he wanted to make sure nothing weakens his resolve. Channa and Siddhartha galloped all night long away from the city. At the dawn, they dismounted in the forest, Channa begged his master to allow him to go with him, but Siddhartha refused. Siddhartha took out his jewelry and other valuables and handed it over to Channa. He cut his hair with sword and became the Monk in quest of the Truth. With heavy heart, Channa returned to Kapilavastu along with rider less Kantaka, to convey the message to the King Suddhodana that his son has become "Sanyasi". King Suddhodana was in an utter shock, he murmured "I did my best Mahamaya, nothing in the world could save our son from the astrological predictions"

The Buddhahood

After leaving his summer palace, Buddha went to the Rajagriha, the capital city of Magadha kingdom. He learned Yoga, Vedas, Upanishads and religious instructions from two renowned Brahmin teachers Alara Kalama and Uddaka Ramaputta. After 6 years of study Siddhartha realized he still not yet achieved the highest level of knowledge so he left the great teachers to continue the quest alone in the year 532 BCE. Siddhartha lived in the dangerous forests and wild places including burial grounds. He neglected completely his surroundings and starved himself of food. One day Siddhartha fainted and fell on the ground, he was too exhausted to move and might have lain there until he died. Luckily, a goat-keeper was passing by and he saw the fallen Siddhartha, the boy bought the she-goat and squeezed few drops of milk from goat's udder into Siddhartha's mouth. The warm goat-milk showed a magical reviving effect on Siddhartha and he could sit up. This was the first practical lesson he learned in the outside world, he realized that the strong and healthy body was necessary to enable unclouded thinking process. Siddhartha finally reached a place called Buddha Gaya (present day, state of Bihar, India), while sitting under a Bodh (bo) tree he decided not to rise out of meditation until he reached the Nirvana. First, he defeated the demonic armies of Mara, lord of illusion, who sought to break his concentration. After the Mara vanished, during the night, he passed through higher levels of awareness based on what he learned from his previous teachers, but he didn't stop there as his teachers did, we went on passing the higher and higher levels of consciousness. At this point, Siddhartha experienced the Great

Enlightenment (Buddhahood), which revealed the way of salvation. Goutham Buddha, finally grasped Four Noble truths:

1. Everyone is struggling for existence and suffering from the fears of Old age, Sickness and Death.
2. Suffering is caused by the ignorance and attachment.
3. By altering the way of life one can pass beyond suffering.
4. The overcoming is achieved through the Noble Eightfold path. (pretty much like Upanishad or Vedanga teachings)

The eight-fold paths are: 1) Right Understanding 2) Right Motives 3) Right Speech 4) Right action 5) Right Occupation 6) Right Endeavor 7) Right Mindfulness 8) Right Meditation

Illustration 9.3: Attainment of Buddhahood and defeat of Mara
(reproduced from MAGADHA Architecture & Culture, 1942)

He stayed near the Bodh tree for a while to avoid any temptations and then decided to preach his discoveries. He first set out for a deer park in Sarnath (Benares) where he met his five former associates. He preached his first sermon to them, it's called 'The Turning of the Wheel of the Law' (Dhamma). Dhamma is a Pali word and its same as Dharma in Sanskrit.

Buddha as a Spiritual Teacher

Side by side with another great religious teacher of Jains (Mahavira), Buddha taught his Dhamma at Rajagriha for 45 years. He converted the Magadha to his own faith of Buddhism. The three great leaders of Jatilas (Brahmanical Vanaprasthas) named Nadi Kassapa, Uruvela Kassapa and Gaya Kassapa and thousands of Jatilas were Buddha's disciples. Buddha preached King Bimbisara and his queen Kshema about his new-found knowledge at the "Venuvana" (Bamboo Grove, as shown in the upper left of Illustration 9.5).

Ac described in the Magadha history books, the "Karanda Venuvana Vihara" which had great baths and a monastery and the garden was watered by perennial springs from Vaibharagiri was consecrated to the Buddha by the King Bimbisara. Buddha converted thousands of people of Magadha to Buddhism; his followers include royal officers of King Bimbisara, noblemen, bankers, traders, daivajnas (astrologers) and even Brahmins. The richest banker of Sravasti named Sudatta Anathapindika met the Buddha at Rajagriha and invited him with all his thousands of disciples to visit Sravasti.

Illustration 9.4: Emperor Asoka (**273-236 B.C.E**), second from left, praying **"Buddham Sharnam Gachhami"** to Bodhi Tree under which Siddhartha experienced the Great Enlightenment to become Buddha (©ASI). The 900-ton granite Sanchi Stupa built on top of the hill during the 2nd Century BCE by the Satavahana rulers; one of the greatest marvels of the world, the statue located at Sanchi, Madhya Pradesh, India

Illustration 9.5: Map of Rajagriha, where Buddha spent 45 years as a
Spiritual Teacher

(reproduced from MAGADHA Architecture & Culture, 1942)

Whenever in Sravasti Buddha stayed at "Vihara of Jetavana" which was
presented to him by Anathapindika. One messenger from his homeland
Kapilavastu came to persuade the Buddha to revisit his place of birth

(Illustration - 9.6). His wife (Yasodhara) and foster-mother (Mahapajapati Gotami) and several ladies adopted Buddhism. Per the works of Malati Madhava, the talented Bhikkunis of that age had a great influence on the society.

Illustration 9.6: Buddha returning to Kapilavastu
(Sanchi – 2nd Century BCE ©ASI)

Although Buddha denied the authority of Vedas, the soul of his teachings was systemized by the philosophy of the Upanishads. That same Vedic philosophy largely influenced the millions of Buddhists and it made Buddhism a world religion. The Buddha attained "Parinirvana" after consuming wild mushroom soup in 487 BCE at Kusinagara. The four famous trees. describe the history of Shakyamuni

(Sage of Sakyas, another name for Buddha). The first tree in Lumbini Park (bordering India and Nepal), where he was born under a tree. The second one is the Bodhi tree at Bodhi Gaya. Buddha attained enlightenment (became Buddha) beneath this Bodhi tree. The third one is in the deer park, under a tree he proclaimed "Dhamma" (his first Sermon). Finally, he attained Mahaparinirvana (final decease) under the Sal-tree at Kusinagara.

Illustration 9.7: Buddha statue at Lumbini park, Hyderabad, Telangana, India
(courtesy © Alosh Bennett)

The tallest Monolithic Buddha

The world's tallest monolith statue of Gautama Buddha located in the middle of a lake at Lumbini Park, Bhagyanagar, Telangana, India. This 58 feet (18m), 350 tons, white granite rock statue was the brain child of then Chief Minister of the erstwhile Andhra Pradesh N.T. Rama Rao (popularly known as NTR). NTR, the demi-God of Andhras, the world record holder for forming a brand new Political Party and winning the election in such a short span of time (9 months). No-single person in the world history of Democracy has ever achieved this kind of political victory other than NTR.

When NTR visited the New York city, he was inspired by the statue of Liberty and wanted to build something similar in his own city. After a long search, he found a solid white granite rock near Raigiri, Bhongir (Nalgonda District, Telangana, India). In October 1985, NTR inaugurated the work on the structure, after five years of work, with the help of hundreds of skilled and semi-skilled workers, the world-famous Temple Architect S.M. Ganapati Sthapati created the Buddha statue. As per NTR, he chose to depict Buddha because "Gautama Buddha was a humanitarian who told the whole truth to the world". The transportation and erection of the statute was not an easy task, it took more than two years and costed 10 lives, finally installed the statue (Illustration 9.7 & 9.8) on December 1, 1992 by the ABC limited, a local company with the help of Japanese technology.

The Dalai Lama (the President of Tibet govt-in-exile, the spiritual leader of Tibetan Buddhism, a Noble Laureate) consecrated the statue after performing a ritual in the year 2006. If you look at the history of the Buddhism, it was popularized by the political class rather than the religious or spiritual leaders. The Emperor Asoka (Illustration 9.4) was responsible for the growth and propagation of Buddhism in India, Sri

Lanka, South China, Tibet, Cambodia, Nepal, Thai, and various other Modern Theravada countries. Unfortunately, the Buddha completely disappeared from India more than 1000 years ago, but NTR re-ignited the Buddhism in India by installing the world's tallest monolithic statue at Lumbini Park (Hussain Sager lake), Hyderabad, Telangana, India.

Illustration 9.8: Standing Buddha at Hyderabad (courtesy ©Shahinamalick)

10. Jesus Christ - The Incarnate Son of God

O Lord, rebuke me not in thy anger,
Nor chasten me in thy wrath.
(Old Testament – Psalms 6:1)

A soft answer turns away wrath,
But a harsh word stirs up anger.
(Old Testament – Psalms 15:1)

Chronology

5 BCE	Birth of Jesus Christ (estimated)
April, 4 BCE	Death of Judean King Herod the Great, the puppet of brutal Roman empire who ordered killing of all infants below the age of two born in Bethlehem. This was to kill Jesus who believed to be born to virgin Mary and the line of descent tracing back to the King David.
30 CE	Crucifixion of Jesus Christ.
46 CE	St. Thomas, one of the twelve apostles of Jesus Christ, suffered martyrdom on the Malabar coast (near Chennai) in Southern India. Based on the inscription found in the year 1857 in North-west India, a general at the court of the King Gudnaphar, called Mazdai (probably referring to some South Indian King) ordered the soldiers to slay Thomas for converting the King's wife Terthia.
64 CE	Large scale persecutions of Church in Rome, the Emperor Nero blamed Christians for the Great Fire of Rome.
68 CE	Ten thousand Jews from Palestine affiliated to Persian Church founded by St Thomas arrived on the Malabar Coast, India.
190 CE	Christian Church built on the Malabar coast near Madras (now Chennai), India
301 CE	Armenia, first country to recognize Christianity as the State religion

313 CE	Constantine-I issues an edict of tolerance to end State persecution of Christians. That was the turning point and the great victory for Christianity.
325 CE	First council of Nicaea, the ecumenical council to settle the Arian dispute concerning the nature of Jesus Christ, convened by the Roman emperor, Constantine-I
354 – 430 CE	St Augustine of Hippo, a vigorous advocate of Roman Catholicism and developed many of his doctrines on Christian theology
Feb 27, 380 CE	Roman empire Theodosius-I declares Nicene Christianity as the state Religion
428 CE – 431 CE	Nestorianism, The Orthodox doctrine that claims Jesus has two natures, one human and one divine, espoused by the Archbishop of Constantinople, Nestorius.
787 CE	Second Council of NICAEA, attended by 350 Bishops. It was convened by Empress Irene. The council restored and validated the veneration of images in the churches throughout the Roman Empire.
1517 CE	Protestant Reformation, initiated by Martin Luther, German religious reformer.
1478 CE - 1535 CE	Sir Thomas More, English writer and Statesman Known for his religious stance against King Henry VIII request for divorce from Catherine of Aragón, it costed his life.

1534 CE	Henry VIII becomes the head of the Anglican Church in England, removed the ecclesiastical authority of Pope over the English church.
Sept 25, 1555 CE	Peace of Augsburg, a proclamation to end war between Lutherans and Roman Catholics in Germany.
Aug 24, 1572 CE	Massacre of St Bartholomew's day; around 100,000 Huguenots (Protestants from France) killed by the Roman Catholic faction.
1618 – 1648 CE	Thirty Years religious war in Germany
Oct 24, 1648 CE	Peace of Westphalia, a treaty signed to end Thirty Years' War.
1649 CE	End of Civil war in England, execution of Charles-I, for treason by the Parliament. The King of England and head of the Church was beheaded in public, outside the Banqueting House near Whitehall, in Westminster, London.
1693 CE	Jakob Amman, a Swiss Mennonite bishop took a stronger stance on doctrine of social shunning which led to formation of Amish branch of Anabaptism. The descendants of Amish who migrated to America in 18th century are called Pennsylvania Dutch. The conservative Amish have always maintained distinctive pastoral life style and they refuse to take part in voting and
1740 CE	Great Awakening, inspired by the preaching of several minsters such as Jonathan Edwards, Gilbert Tennent, and George Whitefield, revival of evangelical religion in the American colonies.

1729 CE	Methodism, founded by the Oxford student John Wesley and his brother Charles Wesley. The Methodist theology leaned heavily on Arminianism and rejected emphasis on "Predestination".
July 14, 1833 CE	Oxford movement (Tractarianism), John Keble, professor of Oxford University initiated the movement with a sermon "On the National Apostasy"
1830 CE	Mormonism, founded by an American Joseph Smith. Its main doctrine assumed that Christianity was corrupt, need to re-establish the divine sacerdotal authority of the ancient Apostles'. It was not clear how this could be achieved because it required new divine initiative or new revelation from the God.
1801 CE – 1877 CE	**Brigham Young**, Second President of Mormons, the colonizer of Utah. He founded the great Salt Lake City in July, 1847. An open advocate of doctrine of Polygamy. He married 27 times and survived by 17 wives and 57 children.
1957 CE	Formation of Southern Christian Leadership Conference (SCLC), an organization devoted to achieving equality for blacks in America. It was formed after the bus boycott in Montgomery, Alabama by **Martin Luther King**, **Jr**. (President of SCLC), Ralph Abernathy, Ella Baker, Andrew Young, and Jesse Jackson.
1960 CE	Nashville Student Movement led by **John Lewis** president of the SNCC (Student Nonviolent Coordinating Committee).

August 28, 1963	The Great March On Washington, one of the largest political rallies in the United States on human rights led by **John Lewis**, demanding jobs and Freedom. SCLC president Martin Luther King Jr., delivered his famous "**I Have a Dream**" speech standing in front of Lincoln Memorial.
1910 CE – 1997 CE	Mother Teresa, Albanian born Indian Roman Catholic Nun; popularly known as Saint Teresa of Calcutta.
Sep 3, 2016 CE	Then Republican Presidential Nominee **Donald J Trump** (now President of United States of America) makes a historical visit to a black Church "Great Faith Ministries", Detroit, Michigan, USA. This was an effort to outreach the black community that has been neglected by the successive American Presidents for more than a half century.
Sep 4, 2016 CE	Vatican declares a nun from Calcutta, Mother Teresa, as the Saint.

What is resurrection theory?

The central theme of the Christianity doctrine is the resurrection of Jesus. According to which Jesus gave the hope of life after the death in the Kingdom of heaven, he did it by rising from the death. But, what if he didn't rise from the death? Then all bets are off, all the teachings about the Christianity should be re-written. Apparently, there were twelve incidents or eye witnesses, twelve apostles of Jesus who confirmed at that time that Jesus indeed rose from the death. Jesus spent 40 days arguing his disciples to go around the world, and baptize people in the name of the Father, the Son, and the Holy Spirit (Matthew 28:19).

The Catholic Church stated in Catechism:

"Although the Resurrection was an historical event that could be verified by the sign of the empty tomb and by the reality of the apostles' encounters with the risen Christ, still it remains at the heart of the mystery of faith as something that transcends and surpasses history"

According to a national survey conducted by the Scripps Survey of Research Center at Ohio University only 36% percent of the people nationwide said they believed in personnel resurrection and the remaining 64% didn't believe at all. Despite large scale disbelief in the resurrection of Jesus Christ, Christianity is still the world's largest religion. Anywhere from 2.2 to 2.4 billion people worldwide follow Christianity. It's quite a remarkable achievement, no other God or Goddess attained this kind of popularity in the history of mankind.

The following table (10.1) shows the summary of beliefs of various sects in Christianity:

Sect of Christianity	Believe in Creeds (Confession)	Salvation	Belief in Trinity	Belief in resurrection of Jesus
Roman Catholics	Yes	exercise of Free will	No	Yes
Eastern Orthodox	Yes		No	
Oriental orthodox	Yes		No	
Methodists	Yes		Yes	Yes
Presbyterians	Yes		Yes	Yes
Congregationalists	Yes		Yes	Yes
Protestants	No	Unmerited Favor	Yes	Yes
Lutherans	Yes	Unmerited Favor	Yes	Yes
Liberal Christians	Yes		Yes	Yes
Modern Christians	Yes		Yes	Yes
Unitarian Universalism	Yes		No	Yes
Jehovah's Witnesses	Yes		No	Yes
Mormonism	Yes		No	Yes

Table 10.1: Showing the differences in various Creeds of Christianity

Judea Prophecy a Myth or real?

The King Herod ordered the armed mercenaries to slaughter the infants in the Bethlehem. Because he believed that the new king, the descendant of king David was born, and he must be killed to save the future kingdom. It affected all the children who were two-year-old or below. The mercenaries who were from Greece, Gaul and Syria showed no sympathy towards small children. As per the legend, the Jewish prophets have predicted coming of the new king based on the following five rules[2]:

Prophecy-I: A bright star will appear in the night sky.

(Referring to the appearance of huge comet)

Prophecy-II: A baby will be born in the small town near Bethlehem. Where King David born thousands of years back.

(Referring to either Bethlehem or Galilee, four miles from Nazareth)

Prophecy-III: A child must be the direct descendant of the David.

(probably referring to IVF described elsewhere)

Prophecy-IV: Powerful men from East will arrive to worship new born king.

(This prophecy might be referring to the people within Judea who would arrive enquiring about the king David)

Prophecy-V: New born baby mother must be virgin.

The Prophecy dates back to three thousand years, taking the mythical part out of the equation. When the Jewish Prophecy was made, what could be the meaning of Prophecy-V? There are rare incidents in the history where a baby born to a Virgin. One such example is the birth of Karna to Kunti. It's an Aryan story from Mahabharata that occurred in the 3rd millennium BCE. The King Kuntibhoja was ruler of the Kunti kingdom in ancient India. He named her daughter with the same name as his kingdom, Kunti. When Princess Kunti was a young woman, the Himalayan Sage Durvasa visited the palace. She impressed the visiting Himalayan Sage Durvasas with her singing and dancing talent. Sage Durvasas gave an unusual boon to Kunti, per which she could call any God at any given time to get a son from him. This was probably beginning of the IVF or assisted reproductive technology during ancient times. Per Jane Dixon, an author of 'The Biology of Kundalini', the virgin birth might be possible due to SWE, which releases the hormones during the peak stages of the Kundalini.

When was Jesus Christ Born?

The exact date and time of Jesus birth is unknown at this point of time; more research is needed. The Gospels of Matthew and Luke provide the genealogies of Jesus. It's written based on religious or spiritual point of view. But not much information on the historical chronology of Jesus Christ. Yet, the historians concluded that there might be an error of 4 to 8 years, from the time the chronology of the Christian era reckoned. Based on this, the Jesus Christ might have born anywhere between 8 BCE and 4 BCE. Per the Jewish historian, Flavius Josephus (Antiquities of the Jews, Book XVII). The Judea king Herod the Great, died shortly after the eclipse of moon, but before the Passover. As per the astronomical observations the lunar eclipses occurred on three occasions, on March 23, 5 BCE at 8.52 PM; March 13, 4 BCE at 4:04 PM and January 10, 1 BCE at 1:35 PM. So, the King Herod might have died in Nisan (April), 4 BCE based on the partial eclipse of Moon occurred on March 13, 4 BCE. Which confirms Jesus was not born in the year 4 BCE, but might have born between 5 BCE and 8 BCE. Assuming that the age of Jesus Christ either 35 or 36 when he was crucified, need to work backwards to arrive at the exact year of birth.

The Judea King Herod wouldn't have sent his mercenaries to kill the infants, unless he was certain that all the five things mentioned in the Jewish prophecy took place. We already have enough information to confirm that Jesus was born sometime between 8 BCE and 4 BCE. Based on the death of Herod occurring in Nissan (April), 4 BCE, the range of search can be further narrowed down to 8 BCE to 5 BCE. Apart from the gospel sources, there are several non-Christian proofs available to confirm the historical existence of Jesus.

Evidence 1: Based on the inscription of Pontius Pilate

In the year 1961, the "Pilate Inscription" partially damaged stone block was accidentally discovered by Italian archaeologists led by Dr. Antonio Frova in the northern coastal city of Caesarea Marittima. The stone was used many times but the Pontius Pilate name is still intact as shown in the illustration 10.1. The partial inscription reads (conjectural letters in brackets): [*Studying the historical Jesus: evaluations of the state of current research* by Bruce Chilton, Craig A. Evans 1998 ISBN 9004111425 page 465]

[*DIS AUGUSTI*] S TIBERIÉUM
[*...PO*] NTIUS PILATUS
[*...PRAEF*] ECTUS IUDA[*EA*]E
[*...FECIT D*] E[*DICAVIT*]

The translation from Latin to English for the inscription reads:

To the Divine Augusti [this] Tiberieum

...Pontius Pilate

...prefect of Judea

...has dedicated [this]

This inscription shows that the historical existence of Judea governor. The new testament mentioned name, Pontius Pilate, who ordered the execution of Jesus Christ. Historians confirmed Pilate was the governor of Roman province of Judea from 26 CE to 36 CE.

Illustration 10.1: Pilate Inscription (Photo Credit @ Caesarea Maritima, Israel)

Evidence 2: Based on the Chinese Astronomical observations

Per the "Quarterly Journal of the Royal Astronomical society", 1991 (Volume 32). The Chinese astronomers recorded the sui-hsing (the long comet) on March, 5 BCE. It appeared in the Capricorn region of the night sky and it lasted for 70 days. The Chinese were correct with a margin of error of a year or so. That means, the Prophecy-I related to bright star occurred in the year 5 BCE was true. So, Jesus might have born either in the year 6 BCE or 5 BCE and we can safely drop the years 7 BCE and 8 BCE.

Evidence 3: Based on the Tacitus's conformation

The Annals of **TACITUS**, BOOK XV., Rebuilding of the city (English translation) has the following on the page 304 and 305:

"**Christus**, from whom the name had its origin, suffered the extreme penalty during the reign of **Tiberius** at the hands of one of our procurators, **Pontius Pilatus**, and a most mischievous superstition, thus checked for the moment, again broke out not only in Judaea, the first source of the evil, but even in Rome, where all things hideous and shameful from every part of the world find their centre and become popular. Accordingly, an arrest was first made of all who pleaded guilty; then, upon their information, an immense multitude was convicted, not so much of the crime of firing the city, as of hatred against mankind. Mockery of every sort was added to their deaths. Covered with the skins of beasts, they were torn by dogs and perished, or were nailed to crosses, or were doomed to the flames and burnt, to serve as a nightly illumination, when daylight had expired."

Illustration 10.2: Cover page of Latin book 'Taciti

The above description is from the English translation of the original book 'TACITI'. Written in Latin by Tacitus. A famous Roman Historian and Senator (book cover shown in Illustration 10.2). The author refers to Jesus in the name of Christus. He thought its name of an epithet rather than a person. But we now know that he was referring to Jesus. Per the author at the time of the Jesus's death, the Tiberius was an emperor. He ruled during period 14 CE to 37 CE. Pontius Pilate was the procurator (governor) of Judea. He was the governor during 26 CE and 36 CE. This collaborates the date of Jesus's death between 29 CE and 36 CE.

Evidence 4: Based on Astronomy Software Simulations

I have run the Voyager 4.5, the dynamic sky simulator to check if the comets as defined in the Prophecy-I were true.

The comet **2P/Encke** was visible during the September, October and November months of 5 BCE for approximately 70 days (Illustration 10.3 to 10.5). It was huge comet visible at Jerusalem and surrounding cities between 5 am and 6:30 am, before the sun rise. Another comet 5D-Brorsen (Illustration 10.6) was also visible during the month of December, 5 BCE

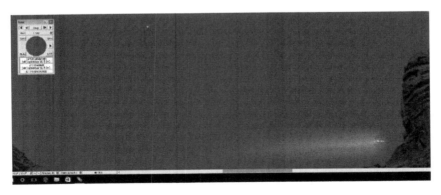

Illustration 10.3: The screenshot of the Voyager Simulator showing the close view of 2P/Enoke comet in the northern horizon near Jerusalem around 5:00 am, on September 28, 5 BCE.

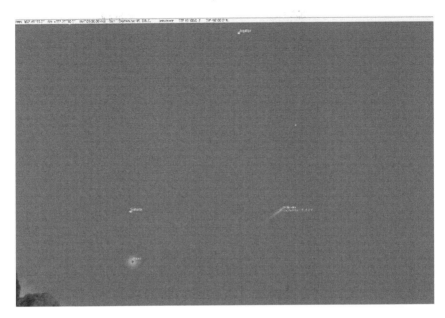

Illustration 10.4: The screenshot of the Voyager Simulator showing the 2P/Enoke comet in the skies near Jerusalem around 5:00 am, on September 15, 5 BCE.

Illustration 10.5: The screenshot of the Voyager Simulator showing the 2P/Enoke comet visible around 5:30 am, near Jerusalem, on November 15, 5 BCE.

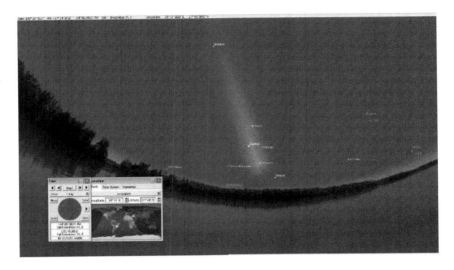

Illustration 10.6: The screenshot of the Voyager Simulator showing the huge comet 5D/Brorsen visible around 5:30 pm, a few minutes after sunset near Jerusalem, on December 31, 5 BCE.

Concluding Remarks:

As per the Jewish historians, the Judea King, Herod died in April, 4 BCE. Based on the Hebrew Calendar, its Nissan, 4 BCE. Which confirms that Jesus was born either in 5 BCE or 6 BCE. Since Jesus was 36 years old at the time of the crucifixion (29 CE), the year of birth should be around 5 BCE. The astronomical software confirmed a huge comet appeared in the northwestern skies of Jerusalem. The comet appeared for more than 70 days, before the sun rise. The appearance of comet corroborates the Judea Prophecy-I. So, the Jesus Christ might have born between September 15, 5 BCE and December 31, 5 BCE (Gregorian Calendar). Based on Hebrew Calendar it's between Tishri 16, 3757 and Tevet 12, 3766.

Any Similarities between Christianity & Vedic Philosophy?

Per Stephen Knapp, in his book "**Proof of Vedic Culture's Global Existence**" (pages 260-262) wrote the following:

".. By studying the teachings that are ascribed to Jesus, we can easily recognize that the essence of what Jesus taught was an elementary level of Bhakti-Yoga and Karma-Yoga. He taught that everyone should love God with their whole heart and mind, which is the quintessence of bhakti-yoga ... As stated in Matthew (22.36-40): "Master, which is the greatest commandment in the law? He answered, Love the Lord thy God with all your heart, with all your soul, with all your mind. This is the greatest commandment. It comes first. The second is like it: Love your neighbor as yourself. Everything in the Law and the prophets hang on these two commandments." These two rules are the heart of the process of Bhakti and Karma-yoga... Jesus also taught that one is judged by his works as the way they behave. This is also the same process as found in bhakti and karma-yoga...

.. the words of Jesus from the Bible that explain that he taught only what God had spoken and was not himself God, but was the son of God the Father. Furthermore, in Bhagavad-Gita (9.17), Krishna specifically explains that He is the Father of all living entities, and (BG 7.6, 10.8) is the origin of all that is material and spiritual. So, no contradiction exists in the understanding that Jesus was a son of God, and Krishna is the supreme Father and Creator of all. In this way, we can see that the essence of Christianity is the basic teachings of the Vedic philosophy. And we can understand the deeper aspects of such knowledge by studying the Vedic texts directly.

It appears that Jesus Christ was dealing with the primitive people of that era. All he needed was to teach them some basic yoga principles (Karma, Bhakti and Maya yoga), which were explained in the Vedic literature. Jesus taught his dispels what God had already taught him. And he gave all the credit to God as mentioned in the Gospel teachings (St. John 5.19, 8.28 & 14.28). "

Section – III

(Anti-Gods)

11. Mahabali

May thy heart be full of generosity,
Kindness and love;
May is flow to the down-trodden
And make them happy!

(Sama Veda 5.5)

Chronology

11,000 BCE	Mahabali scarified his Kingdom to the Vamana and immigrated to the South America. The southern hemisphere was referred to as Pathalam in the Puranas.
800 CE	Beginning of Onam festival.

The Greatest Daithya King

As per the Puranic records Bali Chakravarty (Mahabali) was one of the greatest daithya (asura) kings who always followed the path of Dharma (Truth & Righteous). Mahabali was the powerful Asura king in the Treta yuga and ambitious to rule the entire world. Mahabali, the grandson of Prahalada and Virochana, was a great ruler. The people were happy and prosperous in his rule. Mahabali conquered three Lokas with his mighty power driven out the Devas to the forests. There is another symbolism of the three Lokas, the Hindustan (north India above Vindhyas), Deccan and South India. He was also a great devotee of Lord Vishnu, and everyone (sages, devas and asuras) praised him for this. Per the Hindu legend, the Bali Padyami, the first day of the Kartika Maasa, is the day on which presumably Mahabali rules the world with the blessings of Lord Vishnu. The people of the South-western Indian state of Kerala (called as Keralites) celebrate, a harvest festival "**Onam or Thiru-Onam**" on this Homecoming day of Mahabali.

One of the main motives of Mahabali was to show the entire world that the asuras are good at heart too and need not afraid of them. Mahabali teamed up with the Danava (Asura) Sage Shukracharya and conquered three worlds. The first one is the Earth above equator which belongs to the Manavas (humans). The second one is paathalam, the demon kingdoms below equator. And the third one is Indraloka (the abode of Indra and the sages), the Himalayan kingdom. The other symbolism of the three loka was the Kingdoms above Vindhyas (North India), below Vindhyas (Deccan & East India) and South India.

The Keralites celebrate Onam with pomp and splendor during the Malayalam month called "Chinga Masam"; it normally comes during the period mid-August to mid-September. The celebration starts Ten days prior (called as Atham day) to the actual Thiru-Onam day. The Pookalam (a flower decoration) is laid in front of every house to welcome the vanquished emperor Mahabali; the traditional Dance Kathakali and rituals are performed followed by 'Sadhya' (feast) signifying the Malayalam phrase "Kaanam Vittum Onam Unnanam" meaning everyone should enjoy sumptuous meal on this day of Onam. The main attraction of Onam is the 'Vallamki' (boat race) conducted in the costal shores of Kottayam, Karuvatta, Payippad and Aranmula; hundreds of oarsman row traditional snake boats called 'Chundans' on this day.

Per the historians, the custom of Onam might have started somewhere around **800 CE.** And it's the most important festival to honor the great King Mahabali. There is a powerful myth in existence, even today in several parts of India, succinctly the Vedic god Indra and other devas plotted against Mahabali to send him to Pathalam (below equator, present day South America) to liberate Swargaloka (adobe of Devas, somewhere in the Himalayas). However, the Lord Vishnu allowed him to return to his Kingdom once in a year during the Onam time.

Vamana – Fifth Avatar of Vishnu

The defeat at the hands of the asura king was an embarrassment to the Devas, they pleaded with the Lord Vishnu to help regain the Swargaloka from Bali. The direct fight with the Bali was impossible to win. So, the Sages come up with an indirect method. Where Vishnu transformed into the dwarf (Vamana) and play with his weakness. After driving out the Devas to forest, Mahabali was performing the Ashwamedha Yagna on the banks of Narmada river. As per the Hindu Mythology, Mahabali had to perform just one more Yagna. So, that he could be crowned with the 'Indra' title (king of the gods). While the Yagna was in the final stage and about to complete. Vamana approached the Bali and the generous king got up and invited the Vamana to the Yagna.

Illustration 11.1: Mahabalipuram temple – Maha Vishnu in the Vamana avatar, 7th century CE Granite Statue (courtesy: Archeological Society of India)

Despite the warnings from the Shukracharya, Mahabali promised the Vamana. Per which Mahabali committed to fulfil whatever the dwarf wishes. Vamana told Bali to grant him three steps of land measured by his feet. Bali granted his wish thinking that it's just three yards of land. Again, the Sage Shukracharya tried to stop him. But the Emperor

Mahabali didn't pay attention. The King was about to wash the feet of the Vamana, which was a customary process to fulfill his wish.

Immediately, the dwarf Vamana grew into a giant size and occupied the earth and sky with two feet. And asked Bali to show him a place where to keep the third step. By now, Bali realized that it's a trick played by the Devas. And he determined to keep the promise against all odds, so he offered his head. Vamana placed his foot on the Bali's head and pushed him to the Paathalam (below the earth). There after the Paathalam became the inhabitance of the asuras.

A Better Theory on Vamana

The Vedic Sages and Indra created an avatar called Vamana (dwarf incarnation). They intended to use the weapon of deceit to exploit the genericity of Bali to regain the Swargaloka. The symbolism of the Swargaloka here is the Himalayan territory above the Vindhyas. To fulfill his promise, Bali and his associates migrated to the South America. A place below equator and settled there. The meaning of the Pathalam is anything below the equator.

Illustration 11.2: Lord Vishnu in Vamana Avatar sending Bali to Patalaloka –
7th – 8th Century CE (courtesy - ASI)

The astronomical references found in the Puranas, and the archeological findings in Brazil and Peru prove something. The Bali immigration incident a historical fact. It might have happened sometime between 17, 000 BCE and 11, 000 BCE. Per the Dr. P.V. Vartak, the Daithya King Bali went to South America in 17000 BCE. when the vernal equinox at Jyeshta Moola (Thrikettai or Kettai) Nakshatra. Here is the quotation of Dr. P.V. Vartak available on the web:

"In Vastava Ramayan I have shown that Bali, the demon king went to south America during 17000 BC when the vernal equinox was at Moola Nakshatra. MLBD Newsletter Oct. 1988 gives a news thus: "Dravidians in America" - Per a press report the Brazilian nuclear physicist and researcher Arysio Nunes dos santos holds that the Dravidians of Southern India reached America much before Christopher Columbus. Mr. Nunes dos Santos, of the' Federal University of Minas Gerais maintains that the Dravidians colonized a vast South American region 11000 years before the Europeans reached the new world. Vestiges of the Dravidian presence in America, he says, include the strange phonetics of Gourani, Paraguay's national language. Moreover, Bananas, Pine Apple, Coconut and Cotton, all grown in India could have been taken to America by those navigators."

A Much Better Theory

As per the Rig Veda, Lord Vishnu was identified with the planet Mercury. During the Vedic times, Sages considered him as a lower god and the younger brother of Sun god Indra. As described in Rig Veda (RV 1.154, RV 1.55, RV 1.155 and RV 7.99), the most significant feature of the Lord Vishnu was the measurement of the whole Universe with three steps. The two steps are visible which represent Earth and Sky, but the third step is intangible to the people on the earth. The Symbolism of the three steps of Vamana was related to the rotation of Mercury in our Planetary System. In a calendar year, the planet Mercury makes three rotations around the Sun, so the Sages attributed this celestial phenomenon to the story of dwarf Vamana, who tricked the Emperor Bali on his weakness of gratuitous oath and finally drove him out of the Southern India?

12. Ravana -The Demon King

"The boar knows the plant; the mongoose knows the remedial herb. What the serpents, the gandharvas know, those I call to aid"

(Atharva Veda VIII, 7, 24)

Chronology

7th April, 7307 BCE   Rama-Seeta Kalyanam* (Wedding)

29th Nov, 7306 BCE   Rama, Sita & Lakshmana go into exile

7292 BCE   **Ravana** abducts Princess Seeta in the disguise of saint; failed attempt by demi-god Jatayu, a friend of Dasharatha (Rama's father) to stop Ravana from kidnapping Sita in his Puspakavimana.

1st Sept, 7292 BCE   The Giant Vanara Hanuman enters Lanka and meets Seeta in the Ashoka vanam

Sept/Oct 7292 BCE   Construction of Nala Seetu, as per the Valmiki Ramayanam, the bridge was built in 5 days, on average of 20 Yojanas a day. The dimensions of the bridge 100 Yojanas in length and 10 Yojanas in width; 1 kilometer is approximately equal to 3.5 Yojanas; the Yojana has a different conversion factor in different Yugas, so it's a not a standard unit in the Puranas.

3rd Nov 7292 BCE   Rama-Ravana War begins

7th Nov, 7292 BCE   Kumbahakarna Killed in the war

15th Nov, 7292 BCE   Rama kills Ravana and avenges the great injustice done to Seeta

16th Nov - 6th Dec, 7292 BCE   Seeta undergoes an ordeal of fire to prove her innocence (Agni pariksha)

6th Dec, 7292 BCE   Rama, Seeta, Laxmana and Vibhushan returns to Ayodhya in Puspakavimanam

May/July, 7291 BCE   Despite Agni pariksha, Rama once again sends Seeta (pregnant with twins Kusha & Lava) to forest and instructs Lakshmana to kill her, citing the opinion of his subjects as the reason. Lakshmana didn't have the heart to kill mother like Seeta and he drops her in the forest and tells Rama that job accomplished; Seeta takes refuse at Valmiki Ashram.

7282 BCE - 7279 BCE Lava & Kusha stops Rama's Ashvamedha and defeats his army; Rama invites Seeta to Ayodhya; Seeta refuses but lets her sons Lava and Kusha to go with Rama; after Kusha & Lava left for Ayodhya Seeta ends her life to meet her celestial mother. Rama didn't live long after Seeta's death, he drowned himself in the river Sarayu.

2387 BCE The Splendid capital of Ravana 'Sri Lankapoora' along with several adjoining islands drowned into the Indian Ocean, the exact cause is unknown at this point of time, it might have happened either due to an asteroid impact or due to the plate tectonic activity

1243 BCE Valmiki Ramayana composed into text form from oral format.

544 BCE Wijaya (Vijaya), a member of North Indian Royal clan, who was expelled from the country for his misdeeds by his own father and King, migrates to Ceylon and forms first modern dynasty.

*sources: Bharat, Nepal and Cingalese records; Dr. P.V. Vartak publications and other web sources

Lanka - A paradise on Earth

An island nation Lanka (present name Sri Lanka) was once the richest country, and the most advanced civilization existed here during the Treta Yuga. The Lanka city, built by the legendary architects Vishwakarma and Maya on the top mount Trikuta, a peak of Mahameru. Vishwakarma was the architect for devas. Whereas Maya was an architect for both devas and asuras. In the beginning, Lanka was the home to the Kubera, the richest god of the Treta yuga. But, Ravana threatened his cousin Kubera and took away his kingdom along with his Pushpak Vamana (an ancient flying machine).

Per "Ravana The Great: King of Lanka", 1928, written by Prof. M.S. Purnalingam Pillai ...

"Lanka was also the name of the city of Ravana. It was securely built by the divine architect on the summit of Tirikuta, it was a hundred leagues long and twenty wide. It had stately domes and tall turrets, encircled by a wall built of blocks of gold, and by moats whose waters were bright with lily blossoms. The stately mansions rose like pale-hued clouds in the autumn skies; there were streets broad and bright, gates rich with the sheen of burnished gold ... the Palace looked so glorious that it matched in show an earthly paradise."

History of Ceylon

At the beginning of the time, Lanka known as Ilankai, a province of Tamil-aham, a part of the main land of India. It was during the Sangam era, somewhere around 8,000 BCE, the glaciers meltdown. Aftermath of the ice age raised the sea levels by 400 feet. And this submerged the portions of mainland India connecting the Ceylon. From that point onwards Ceylon lost all the land routes until Sri Rama built the Nala Ketu in the Treta yuga.

Illustration 12.1: Puranic imaginary map of India where Lanka was part of Southern India (source: Ravana The Great: King of Lanka, M.S. Purnalingam Pillai, 1928)

The 'Tamprobane' was the name given by the Megasthenes. The Greek Ambassador, presumably sent by the Seleukos Nicator of Syria. He visited the rajyashabha of the emperor Chandragupta, the grandfather of the emperor Asoka. The Arabs called Ceylon Serendib and the Portuguese called it as 'Ceilao'. But it's known as the Lanka to the people of main land India for several thousands of years before the Christian era. The Rakshasas who existed in the Lanka during the Treta yuga were neither Tamils nor Sinhalese. They were the aboriginal Dravidians and who speak Dravidian. The language precursor to Sanskrit and no longer spoken in the present-day Sri Lanka. The Splendid capital of Ravana 'Sri Lankapoora'. Along with several adjoining islands drowned into the Indian Ocean. This incident occurred in the year 2387 BCE. No one knows the exact cause, it was either an Android impact caused it or due to some Plate Tectonic activity.

The Sinhalese, occupying the south were migrated from Bengal about 600 BCE and the Tamils found in Jaffna (north side) were the immigrants from Southern India more than 3000 years back. As per the historical events recorded in the chronicles. Wijaya (or Vijaya) a descendant of a royal family in North India, formed the first dynasty in Ceylon. This event took place in the year **544 BCE**.

Ravana's Lineage

Based on the hoary legend, Ravana was half-Brahmin and half-Rakshasa. And knew the Vedas, might have learned from his father. Per Hindu legend, Ravana born at Devagana. To the demon princess Kaikesi and the great Sage Vishvara. As per the Hindu legend Ravana was the grandson of the sage Pulastya. Who was one of the Ten Prajapatis and one of the seven great sages of Manu, known as 'Saptarishi'. His siblings include Kumbakarna, Vibishana, Ahiravana and Surpanaka. Out of which Vibishana was the only one who defected to the Rama's side.

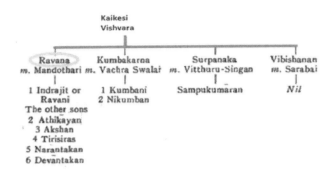

Illustration 12.2: The family tree of Kekasi (redrawn from the source: The Great, King of Lanka", M.S. Purnalingam Pillai)

Why the name Ravana?

The word Ravana means 'roaring' or 'causing to cry', the name given by the Lord Shiva. Per the legendary 6th century CE granite sculpture available at the Ellora caves, Maharashtra (India), Ravana attacked the Alakapuri, near Himalayas, his half-brother Khubera's kingdom and took the flying machine 'Pusphaka Vimana' from him. On the way, back home to Lanka, he stopped at the mount Kailasha, Ravana hurt the Shiva's Nandi which was not letting him go up the hill. This angered Shiva and he captured Ravana and imprisoned him under the mount Khailasa and crashed his toes with Mount Kailash hill rock. Ravana started crying due to unbearable pain and later started singing Vedic hymns to praise Shiva. Lord Shiva was pleased with the hymns, and granted him any boons he wanted. The crooked Ravana requested Shiva to give him the beautiful girl sitting on the top mount Khalish, thinking that she was the wife of Shiva, but she turns out to be none other than the first wife of Ravana Mondadori.

Illustration 12.3: Ravana lifting Khailasa, 6th -7th century CE Ellora caves (courtesy: ASI)

Ravana - Dashakanta

Have you wondered why Ravana had 10 heads? In fact, he didn't have ten heads, he was proficient in 4 Vedas and 6 Upanishads, that's why he was called 'Dashaanan' (ten headed demon), Dashamukha (Ten heads) or Dashakanta. Some people in Sri Lanka consider Ravana with 9 heads which represent the 9 planets because Ravana was a great astronomer. Similarly, the people in Nepal consider him with 12 heads representing the twelve constellations he studied as an astrologer.

Illustration 12.4: Postal stamp of Ravana mask issued by India Post in the year 1974.

Ravana was also considered as the Ashivaka Siddha as he was expert in Music (Veena), Medicine, Political Science, Vedas (siddha) and a warrior with Battle field knowledge. Ravana wrote several books in Medicine and Astronomy; the most popular one is 'Ravana Samhita', its considered as the best work on Hindu Astrology, per some sources the manuscript of this book is still available in the Nepal museum.

Ravana abducts Sita

Due to a dynastic dispute over the succession to the throne, the prince of Ayodhya Rama goes into exile along with his wife Sita and half-brother Lakshmana after learning about the Maharajah Dasaratha's promise to Kaikeyi to crown his step-brother Bhaaratha as the king. Rama performed 'svadharma' by helping his father decision to grant a boon to Kaikeyi (Dasaratha's second wife), this event occurred on 29th Nov, 7306 BCE (per the astronomical dating by Dr. P. V. Vartak; the

Mahabharata Aadiparva (A.71) and Ashwamedha has several references to the Nakshatras of Ramayana era).

Rama, Sita and Lakshmana went deep into the Jungles to find out a suitable place for building a hut, they finally crossed Vindhya Parvathas (Mountains) and entered the Deccan area, south central Bharath. After wandering several places for ten years, on the advice of the sage Agastya, they finally reached a place called Panchavati situated at foothills of the Western Ghats, it's the birth place of Godavari river. That was the place where dangerous rakshasas roam around and destroy the Yagna of sages on frequent basis. The royal exiles built a hut with several rooms and lived there for three and half years, another six months left before they could come out of exile and go back to Ayodhya to reclaim their kingdom.

One fine day, a rakshasa woman approached Rama and introduced herself as the sister of Lanka King Ravana and expressed her love for Rama and proposed to marry him. Rama pointed out at the beautiful woman Sita and told her "Sita is my beloved bride … but Lakshmana … a fit husband for thee". Surpanaka left the place abruptly and approached Lakshmana with the same proposal. But Lakshmana enjoyed jesting with her rather than marrying. The furious Surpanaka sprang towards Sita with an intention to kill her, but Rama thrust her away from Sita. Rama ordered Lakshmana to cut off her ears and nose. Lakshmana was loyal brother; out of his brotherly devotion, didn't even think for a minute, took out the sword and disfigured Surpanaka. Surpanaka went straight to her half-brother Kahara; related him what had taken place. Khara was shocked to see bleeding and mutated Surpanaka, he swore he would avenge her mutation. He took an army of asuras along with him, but Rama alone fought and sent everybody to Yamapuri. Surpanaka hastened to Lanka and told her big brother Ravana, this was the beginning of the war of revenge. Ravana wanted to see the death of Rama and his brother but Surpanaka wanted him to captivate his beautiful wife Sita, Rama could be slayed this way because he couldn't exist without her.

Ravana summoned Maricha, who had an ability to assume any shapes and do the mimicry. On hearing the news Maricha was almost certain that his death in the hands of Rama was certain. Marcia recollected how he narrowly escaped from the deadly arrows of 13-year old boy Rama in the past when he tried to destroy Vishvamitra's Yagna. They flew in Ravana's flying chariot (Puspakavimana) and landed close to the hermitage of the Rama. As per the plot Maricha assumed the shape of a golden deer and attracted the attention of Rama and Sita. Rama told Lakshmana to take care of the hermitage until his return and went after the golden deer to fulfil the desire of Sita.

Rama chased the deer for a long time in the forest, when he couldn't catch it alive, then he shot an arrow which pierced the heart of the deer. Maricha jumped out of the deer's body and shouted in a loud voice imitating Rama's voice "Oh Lakshmana… Oh Sita". On hearing the Rama's voice, Sita became worried and told Lakshmana to find out what happened to Rama. Lakshmana was reluctant in the beginning and told her not to worry about his heroic brother. Later, Lakshmana went to see Rama after hearing the sarcastic words from Sita. Before leaving the hermitage, he drew a Rekha (line) and told her not to cross that at any cost. This Rekha popularly known as "**Lakshmana Rekha**", without this there was no history of Ramayana. Ravana was impatiently waiting outside for the opportunity to grab Sita. Once, Lakshmana left, the Ravana in the disguise of mendicant come in front of the hermitage and shouts "Biksham Dhehe", requesting for food.

Illustration 12.5: Jatayu attacking Ravana to protect Sita
(8th Century CE, Ellora Caves, India ©ASI)

As per the customs of those days, Sita offered him the food from inside the boundary of the **Lakshmana-Rekha**. The Ravana in disguise of mendicant declined to accept the food and asked her to come outside the boundary line and offer him food. Sita hesitated for a minute to cross the Rekha, but the mendicant got angry and admonished her for the rudeness. As per the Rakshasas rules of the Treta Yuga, they have the right to abduct any women found in the forest but not from their homes. Since Ravana was a half-Brahmin, a big question - was he entitled to Rakshasa rules? Once Sita crossed the 'Lakshmana Rekha', Ravana abducted her and flew away in the Puspakavimana (Illustration 12.5). This incident occurred sometime between **7293** BCE and **7292** BCE.

A Lesson to be learned from the history

Sita's story was a story of sacrifice and sorrow to keep alive the dharma of Treta yuga. Sita paid heavy price for crossing the "**Lakshmana-Rekha**". Based on the information he got it from Sages, Lakshmana knew the Rakshasas can't go inside the hermitage and abduct the people. But the Rakshasa rules allow them to grab any women outside her house. That's why he drew a boundary line around the Hermitage (popularly known as "Lakshmana Rekha") to protect Sita in his absence. Some critics drew different conclusions and even went into some greater lengths in ridiculing Laxmana-Rekha as the physical manifestation of the main doorway of an orthodox Hindu house, where woman allowed to cross the doorway only twice, once as a bride on way to her husband's house and the second time as a corpse on her way to the Smashanam (crematorium). It might sound ridiculous, but the Lakshmana-Rekha applies to both male and female, there are dangers everywhere, never cross the lines, pay attention to the details, listen more and listen to your family and well-wishers. This is the basic principle of survival in this dark age of **Kali yuga**.

Finding Sita

After returning from the forest, Rama and Lakshmana shocked to find that the doors of the hermitage were open and Sita not found inside. They quickly realized that Sita was carried away and need to start the search. They searched everywhere in the Dandakaranya, thick forest filled with wild animals and Rakshasas. The first clue they found was from the dying demi-god Jatayu, a raja of vultures, a friend of Dasharatha. The Jatayu intercepted Ravana and fought with him vigorously when heard the cries of Sita, but Ravana cut his both the wings and he was badly wounded, barely waiting for the Rama to convey the message before he dies (Illustration 12.5). Rama and Lakshmana re-started the search and went in the southern direction pointed out by Jatayu. After a few weeks of journey, they ran into a Rakshasa Kabandha, after hearing the story of Sita abduction, he advised them to meet Sugriva who might be available either on the Rishyamukha hill or Lake Pampa. On the way to Pampa Lake, Rama and Lakshmana visited a bright and knowledgeable saint Shabri at the ashram of the sage Matanga, she also advised Rama to take the help of an exile monkey king Sugriva with their search for Sita.

On seeing Rama and Lakshmana on Rishyamukha hill, Sugriva went into hiding, not knowing who they were. Finally, Hanuman met Rama and Lakshmana and brought them to the cave where Sugriva was hiding. Sugriva showed Rama the ornaments they found near the mountain top and Rama recognized it as the jewelry of Sita which further confirmed that Sita was taken in the southern direction.

Sugriva made an alliance with Rama based on a condition that Rama would kill Vali. After the second attempt Rama stuck mighty Vali with an arrow from behind the tree. Vali fell to the ground and before dying he questioned Rama's cowardliness to hit him from behind. Clearly, Rama had no answer other than talking about the alliance he made with Sugriva. After the coronation as the king of Kishkinda, Sugriva forgot about the promise he made to Rama. This angered Rama and Lakshmana, after a prolonged delay the search parties were sent into each direction to look out for Sita. Vinata went in the east direction, Sushena to the west, Shatabali to the north and finally Hanuman and Angada led the search party in the most crucial direction, the south towards Lanka. Rama had a great confidence in Hanuman so he gave him his ring as a proof to show it to Sita whenever he finds her.

All the search parties retuned with empty hands after a month or so, the deadline set by the Sugriva, but the Sothern party led by Hanuman didn't return. They began the search in the thick forests of Vindhya and later stuck for more than a month in the Rikshabila and Swayamprabha valleys. As per Valmiki description the valleys were filled with Sandal wood, fruits and delicious honey, probably referring to present day Kerala or Malabar coast. The search party was totally exhausted and sitting close to the sea shore decided to give up the search and return to Kishkinda. Then a miracle occurred, Sampati, an elder brother of Jatayu arrived at the scene and pointed them towards Lanka where Sita was stationed. Based on the Jambavan's suggestion, Hanuman decided to jump across the sea.

Q. Who is Jambavan and how could Hanuman cross sea?

Author's Theory: Both Jambavan and Hanuman were actually human beings in an animal masks. The masks were probably needed to control and train the Vanara (Money) Army. Hanuman wears the Giant Money

Mask fitted with a flying machine and that's how he could cross the sea to reach Lanka. Based on the description available in Valmiki's Sundara Kanda, Hanuman assumes a minuscule form when he meets Sita in the Ashoka Vanam. This tells us, Hanuman was probably a small person but appeared like a giant money when he wore the mask.

Hanuman climbed to the top of the Mahindra hill and jumped into the sea and then started swimming towards the Lanka. It was a difficult journey for Hanuman, he killed the Surasa, a mother of Nagas and the dragon named Sinhika on his way before he reaching Lanka. Hanuman waited till the night had fallen and then entered Ravana's Mansion. He heard the music played to announce the various phases of the night. Hanuman crept on through the Rakshasa women's chambers, searched through the Ravana's palace everywhere but couldn't find any traces of Sita. Hanuman wandered on throughout night until he reached Asoka-vanam. There he found the long lost Sita surrounded by the deadly she demons.

Hanuman waited till morning and approached Sita, at first Sita was afraid that Ravana assumed monkey form to deceive her but later Hanuman showed her the ring of Rama. Sita was overjoyed to see Hanuman. Hanuman offered to carry away her on his back, but she refused and instead told him to bring Rama within two months, the deadline set by the Ravana to kill her if she failed to yield to him. Sita took out a bright precious jewel from her hair and gave it to Hanuman as a token of appreciation.

Indrajit, son of Ravana captured Hanuman and presented him in front of the Ravana's court. Ravana released Hanuman on the request of Vibishana but ordered to wrap an oil soaked cloth to his tail and set it on fire as a punishment. Hanuman preyed on the situation and caused greater damage, he leapt over the city, setting fire with his flaming tail to the beautiful mansions of Lanka. Hanuman got a chance to meet Sita once again before he joined the Vanara party on the other side of the ocean. Rama rejoiced greatly on hearing the news from Hanuman about his loved one. The preparation to rescue Sita began at once, Rama and Vanara army started marching towards southern direction. Rama and Vanara Army crossed Sahaya mountain range, Malaya mountain range and then the Mahindra mountain range before they reached the southern sea shore.

Q. When you say, Rama and Vanara (Monkey army) went on a war, is it a real history or Chronicles of Narnia Style fantasy Story?

Ramayana story is not historical fiction, it's the real story. Here is an example from the history:

In the olden days, many Indian Kings used to deploy Monkeys and Langurs as the battle soldiers. The last Indian king who used the monkey army was King Purushottama (King Porus as per Greek records). In 327 BCE, King Purushottama's Vanara (Money) Army defeated the Alexander the Great in an unprecedented way as soon as they crossed Jhelum river. Alexander severely injured as the monkeys attacked and dragged him into the forest and everybody thought he was dead. After several months of rigorous struggle Alexander finally survived. The credit goes to a tribal Ayurvedic physician who treated him day and night. After hearing the miraculous survival story, king Purushottama made an alliance and returned the kingdom back to Alexander the Great. Ancient Indian Kings always had the tradition of employing animals as the combatant war soldiers since beginning of the time.

Is Nala Setu man made?

The entire Ramayana can be described in three words in Telugu "Khate, Khote, Theche". The meaning, Rama built the bridge (Khate), killed Ravana (Khote) and brought Sita back (Theche) to Ayodhya. So, the construction of bridge between India and Lanka was always a center piece of Ramayana. There were some arguments, Nala might have used the preexisting limestone base already built by Ravana or naturally occurring geological phenomenon. Whatever it was, whether Nala built from the scratch or used the pre-existing structure as the basis for his construction, "Nala Setu" should be considered as one of the most challenging civil engineering marvels of the ancient times.

During the Pleistocene epoch of the quaternary Ice age, most of the Northen hemispehre (North America & Europe) covered by the glaciers. Some people think we are still in ice age, but the last ice age ended about 10,000 (8,000BCE) years ago, that caused the glaciers to melt down and the sea levels rised upto 400 feet.

Several Southern Indian cities and the landmass between India and Lanka submerged into the ocean. The good news, the next ice age won't occur in the next 150 million years, so do we need to worry about global warming? The calculation is based on combinations of galatic rotation of milkyway galaxy and continental drift etc. The earliest recoded life on the earth, about 3.6 billion years ago, the average surface temperature was 20°C with an uncertainity range of 5°C, the Earth remained free of ice ages for more than 90% cent of the time.

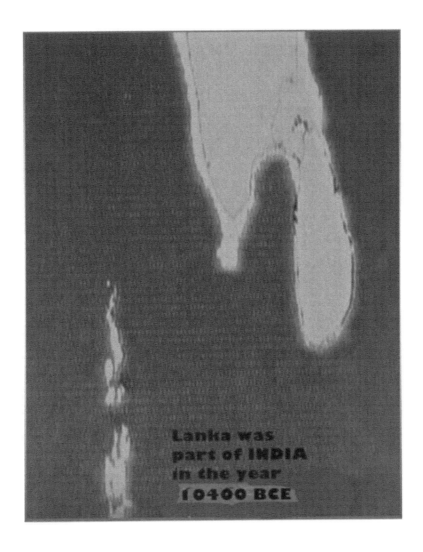

Illustration 12.6: Computer simulation showing the landmass between Lanka and India around 10,400 BCE.

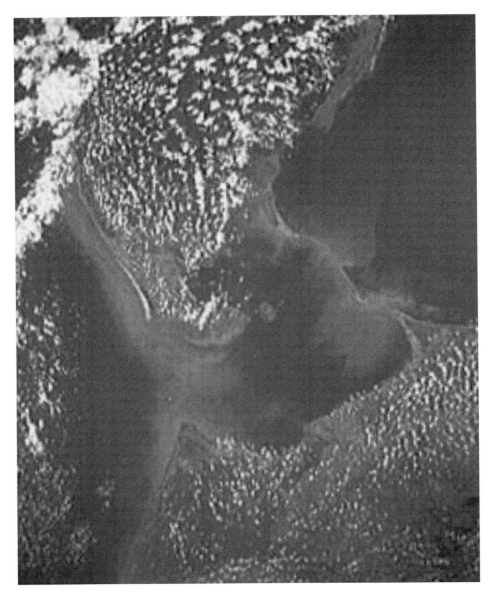

Illustration 12.7: Satellite view of Nala Setu (present day), the bridge is still visible but submerged in the sea due to the substrate accumulation and increase in ocean levels over the period of 9000 years (©photo credit: NASA).

When did Ramayana Happen?

There are some arguments on when did Ramayana happen? Is it 12000 BCE or 7500 BCE or 5500 BCE or even 3500 BCE? I think the 12500 BCE can be easily ruled out without any argument because the Lanka was land locked with India and there wouldn't be any need to construct a bridge (as shown in the computer simulated illustration 12.6). The year 3500 BCE can't be true because the astronomical observations doesn't support this and more ever the "Taittiriya Brahmana (TB)" written in 4600 BCE refers to Valmiki as the adi-kavi (guru) as per Dr. P.V. Vartak, so Ramayana must have happened before TB was composed. As per Valmiki, the Ramayana occurred in the Treta yuga, thus the 5500 BCE can't be true because that period belongs to Dwapara yuga.

A prominent scholar on Hinduism, **Wendy Doniger** quoted a Sufi parable on 'working with available light' in her book "The Hindus, an alternative history" (page. 17), as follows:

"... working with available light ... someone saw Nasrudin searching for something on the ground. "what have you lost, Mulla?" he asked. "My key" said the Mulla. So, they both went down on their knees and looked for it. After a time, the other man asked "Where exactly did you drop it?" "In my own house." "Then why are you looking here?" "There is more light here than inside my house." ... This Sufi parable could stand as a cautionary tale for anyone searching for the keys ... to the history of the Hindus... I have... concentrated on those moments that have been illuminated by the many scholars ..."

On the similar lines, the Ayodhya exists today but the archeological evidence had been long back destroyed by the barbaric invaders, the Lanka exists today but the Ravana's capital city Lankapoora submerged into the ocean more than 5000 years ago, where should we search? The only archeological evidence we have today is the Nala Setu and that is under water too, not because its submerged in the sea but because of the court disputes in the hands of anti-folk ballads. That means, we should search where the light is ... I literally meant where the light is ... yes, where the light house is. There is a light house (**The great Basses**) between Lanka and the Maldives, as per the historians, this used to be there since the beginning of the time and it's still called as Ravana's fort, thus an underwater archeological search about 400 miles from western limit of Ceylon, in the south-east sea of Ceylon should be able to provide the real evidence. Until such time, Dr. P. V. Vartak explanation (as explained in Vastav Ramayanam) makes more sense:

" .... Sage Vishwamitra started counting Nakshatras from Shravana (Aadiparva A.71 and Ashwamedha A.44) and a new reference to time measurement thus initiated. According the old tradition, the first place was assigned to the Nakshatra prevalent on the Vernal Equinox. Vishwamitra modified this and started measuring from the Nakshatra at the Autumnal Equinox. Shravana was at this juncture at about 7500 BCE, which is thus the probable period when Vishwamitra existed and that of Ramayanic Era."

Construction of Nala Setu

After seeing the partial destruction of Lanka by the Hanuman, Ravana held a council of war and sought advice from each member. Prahasta, the prime minster assured that Ravana had nothing to fear, he alone would defeat the Vanaras. All others indulge in similar kind of self-praise and glory of Asura army, except Vibishana who warned his brother against the impending doom and told him to return Sita to Rama immediately and thus avert the catastrophe.

Ravana was furious on hearing the praises about his enemy from his own cowardly brother, he dismissed Vibishana from the council hall. Vibishana fled to the other side of the sea where Rama was, accompanied by his four captains Analan, Anilan, Aran and Sampathi. Sugriva took him for a spy, Angadha and Jambavan expressed similar doubts, but Rama welcomed Vibishana after hearing the praises from Hanuman.

Nala approached Rama and introduced himself as the decedent of the legendary Architect Vishwakarma and explained his skills in bridge construction and asked Rama's permission to construct the bridge. Rama asked the opinion of Sugriva and his new-found ally Vibishana and they all expressed the similar opinion in favor of bridge construction. Nala started the bridge construction with the help of Vanaras. As described in Valmiki Ramayanam, it was a well-planned civil engineering effort, not just a random throwing of stones and trees into the water, Vanaras were holding the ropes for several Yojanas to get the linear alignment. The tree logs (such as Sala, Asvakarna, Dhava, Bamboo, Mango, Ashoka etc.) were used as the base layer and upon which both big and small boulders were laid.

As per Valmiki's description, the bridge measured 100 Yojanas in length and 10 Yojanas in width. This description matches with the present-day Rama Setu (or Adam's bridge) which is 35 Kilometers in length (approximately 100 Yojanas). The bridge was constructed in 5 days, the first day 14 Yojanas, second day 20, third day 21, fourth day 22 and finally 23 Yojanas on the fifth day. Rama was pleased with Nala's efforts in bridge construction, and called it as "Nala-Setu". The Vanara army crossed the bridge and entered the Lanka, they camped on the southern seashore and the war was proclaimed shortly after that.

End of Ravana Regime

Ravana sent two spies Sardula and Suka to survey the enemy's forces. Based on the reports he ordered his generals to secure all the gates of Lanka and be ready for valiant defense. Vanaras marched southward and surveyed the island from the Suvela mountain peak. The war began with exhibition of magic tricks by Ravana's son Indrajit, he defeated both Rama and Lakshmana; they both fainted and fell on the ground. Indrajit thought both the brothers were dead so he returned to Lanka to celebrate the victory with his father Ravana.

In the meantime, Hanuman and other Vanaras surrounded Rama and Lakshmana and guarded their bodies. By end of the day, the Rama and Lakshmana returned to the consciousness, the Vanara army made a tumultuous celebration on seeing both the brothers alive. Ravana was overwhelmed after hearing that Rama and Lakshmana are in good condition, he sent Dhumraksha to lead the army and destroy Rama. Hanuman killed the Dhumraksha and later Angadha killed the Vajradamsha sent by Ravana. Hanuman killed Akampana, the brave and mighty commander of Ravana, the Nila killed the commander-in-chief Prahasta before the end of the day.

Ravana himself went to the war first time, but he was hurt by Rama and he had no option but retreat and return to Lanka. Ravana decided to rouse Kumbhakarna from the sleep. On the next day, Kumbhakarna fought bravely and caused significant damage to the Vanara Army. Both Rama and Lakshmana attacked the Kumbhakarna, Lakshmana destroyed the body armor and the Rama killed Kumbhakarna. On hearing the news about the death of Kumbhakarna, Ravana laments in various ways. The Vanara army killed the brave warriors of Ravana - Narantaka, Devantaka, Trishira, Mahodara, Mahaparshwa and Atikaya.

After hearing the news of enormous destruction, Indrajit consoled his father and vowed to destroy the enemy army. Indrajit went to the battlefield accompanied by the huge army. He caused enormous damage and finally hurt Rama, Laxmana and scores of other Vanara warriors with the Brahma Astra. Because of Brahmastra everybody was unconscious, except Hanuman, Vibishana and Jambavan. Jambavan asked Hanuman to bring the medical herbs from Himalayas.

Hanuman left for Himalayas in the middle of the night via mount Rishabha. He couldn't recognize the specific herbs so he uprooted the whole area and brought it by the early morning on the next day. Many Vanara warriors including Lakshmana were healed by the application of herbs. Vanara army attacked the Lanka city in the night and set ablaze several mansions. They also killed several warriors – Kampana, Prajagnha, shonitaska, Yupaksha, Kumbha and Nikumbha. Rama killed Makarasha, son of Khara. Ravana was furious and he asked Indrajit to lead the battlefield. There was fierce fighting between Indrajit and Lakshmana; Vibhushana acted as a guard and encouraged Vanaras to fight. Lakshmana first killed the charioteer of Indrajit and the Vanaras killed the horses of Indrajit. This left Indrajit hopeless, without his chariot he couldn't play any magic tricks but continued to fight with Lakshmana. At the end Indrajit was killed by one of the arrows aimed by Lakshmana. Rama embraced his brother and praised Lakshmana and Vibhushana for killing the mighty warrior Indrajit.

Ravana was shocked to hear the news of Indrajit's death, he sought a fitting revenge for his brave and noble son, he first wanted to kill Sita but one of his minsters Suprashwa stopped him from doing such a cowardly act and he advised him to go to war himself and take the revenge. Ravana himself marched to the battlefield along with his generals on the next day. Ravana attacked vigorously on the Vanara army and caused much damage. When Ravana noticed that his defected brother Vibishana battling by the enemy's side, he threw a mighty Shula (javelin) at him, but Lakshmana intercepted that and saved him. Ravana threw a Sakti (Tri-Shula, he got it from the Lord Shiva) weapon this time and it pierced Lakshmana and he fell. Hanuman played the Galen he brought the healing herbs, Lakshmana recovered under the treatment of Sushena. Rama was pleased to see Lakshmana back to normal with help of the herbs. The battle between Rama and Ravana started immediately after that. Rama severely attacked Ravana with his arrows, it stuck his chest and forehead. Ravana was severely hurt, Ravana's charioteer took him away from the battlefield.

After a while Ravana recovered and he went back to the battle field for the third time in a new chariot and attacked Rama. At the same time Matali, charioteer of Indra arrived at the battle field to assist Rama. Matali advised Rama to use the Brahma's Divya Astra he got it from the sage Agastya. There was a fierce battle between Rama and Ravana, but Ravana couldn't withstand the dreadful Brahmastra discharged by Rama. It pierced Ravana's heart and laid him down lifeless, that was the end of the war and end of the great regime of Ravana. Mondadori, Ravana's widow wept bitter tears over the dead body of her husband. Hanuman informed Sita about the victory of Rama. Vibhushana performed funeral rites of Ravana according to the Vedic traditions prevailing at that time, with the sacrifice of a goat on **16th Nov, 7292 BCE**.

Vibhushana brought Sita to Rama, Rama instructed him to arrange for the fire ordeal to prove her innocence. This was the most embarrassing moment; Hanuman, Vibhushana, Sugriva and everybody was shocked at the mean act of Rama. But at the end everybody was happy because Sita walked through fire ordeal and easily passed the test. On **6th Dec, 7292 BCE** Rama, Sita, Laxmana accompanied by the Hanuman, Sugriva and other Vanaras left for Ayodhya in a Puspakavimanam (flying vehicle) provided by Vibhushana. On their way back home, Rama showed Sita the aerial view of the bridge they constructed to reach Lanka and praised Nala for the magnificent work he had done in building this and he called it "Nala Setu", dedicating it in the name of Nala.

13. Narakasura – The Demon of Darkness

"That Transcendent One, is
Whom all beings abide, by Whom all
This world is pervaded, may be reached
by unswerving devotion"

-Bhagavad Gita (VIII-22)

[Translated by Chakravarti Rajagopalachari, popularly known as Rajaji, the First Indian Governor General of Independent India and Home Minister of Republic of India]

Chronology

78000 BCE – 74000 BCE   **TOBA** eruption, world's worst volcanic eruption occurred at the present location of Lake Toba, Indonesia. The erupted ash clouds affected the whole south Asia and Indian Ocean.

A Tyrant ruler of Pragjyotishpuram

Narakasura was the tyrant and wicked ruler of Pragjyotishpuram[1]. The Pragyotisa-pura, present day known as the Gouhati, a capital city of Assam, India. He ordered all the people of his kingdom not to lit any lamps either on the streets or in their houses. The Bhagavata describes Narakasura the son of Dharitri (goddess Bhumi Devi, the Earth). He kidnapped 16,000 beautiful princesses and imprisoned them inside his fort. No woman could walk free on the streets; all the inhabitants of the mother Earth became the victims.

Per the Parabola Volume 2.6 series (The Inner Journey – views from the Hindu Tradition) "The Slaying of Narakasura", the following was mentioned to describe the atrocities of the demon Narakasura:

"As his powers and ego increased. Narakasura's nefarious activities began to reach new proportions. He turned his sight toward the heavens and defeated all the gods and their leader, Indra, in the ensuring battle. Adding insult to injury, he seized the famed umbrella of Varuna, snatched the precious earrings adorning Aditi, and occupied Maniparvata, the summit of Mount Mandara. Indra was furious, for Varuna not only the god of water and guardian of the western quarter but also his brother, Aditi was his own mother, and Maniparvata was the favorite resort for the gods. One way or another, the demon had to be stopped."

With an intension to free the world from the clutches of the demon Narakasura, the king of the Gods, Lord Indra approached Lord Krishna at his palace in the mythical city of Dwaraka. Indra requested Lord Krishna to save the world from the atrocities committed by the demon Narakasura. After listening to the misdeeds of Narakasura, Lord Krishna left for Pragjyotishpuram on his flying vehicle (Mythical bird, Garuda) accompanied by his consort, Satyabhāmā.

The Killing of the demon Narakasura

The Pragjyotishpuram, surrounded by the hills and five layers of fortifications. Such as the rings of water, lighting, fire, rain, and wind. The inner circle, surrounded by the obstructions of mura-pasa cables[2]. Designed and guarded by the demon architect 'Mura'. Lord Krishna broke through the rock fortifications with his cudgel. Then his arrows broke the rings of water, fire, wind, and unmanned weapon fortifications. He used the sword to cut the Mura-pasa wires and that gave access to the inner circle.

Illustration 13.1: Lord Krishna battels the Armies of Narakasura (Acknowledged to Delhi-Agra area- The Metropolitan Museum of Art [1])

Lord Krishna blew his 'conchshell' to challenge the Narakasura, a sound as terrifying as the thunder at the end of the cosmic age[2]. The vibrations of the Pancajanya conchshell woke up the five-headed demon Mura who was sleeping at the bottom of the moat. In a fierce battle, Lord Krishna killed the Narakasura's general Mura with his 'Sudharshana

Chakra' (divine discus), and hence earned the name 'Murari' (the destroyer of the demon architect Mura). The seven sons of Mura attacked Lord Krishna with weapons. They are Tamara, Antariksa, Sravana, Vibhavasu, Vasu, Nabhasvan and Aruna. They threw at him arrows, clubs, swords, spears, lances and tridents. They wanted to avenge their father's death. But, Lord Krishna defeated them with his arrows without much difficulty. The Pitha, general of Narakasura, and his huge army of elephants met with the similar type of fate, a one-way trip to the adobe of Yamaraja.

Narakasura, enraged by the fate of his army. He went out of the citadel with elephants born out of the milk ocean to attack Lord Krishna. The Demon Narakasura hit the Lord Krishna with his Sataghani weapon. The impact was so high; Lord Krishna fell unconscious for few minutes. Seeing her husband fell unconscious, Satyabhāmā was furious. She took the arrow and started shooting sharp arrows towards Narakasura. Narakasura didn't expect this, one of the arrow stuck Narakasura and cut off his head. After killing Narakasura, Lord Krishna visited the palace of Narakasura accompanied by Satyabhāmā.

The goddess of Earth, Bhumi Devi invited the divine couple into the palace. She presented them precious gifts and jewels. And returned Aditi's earrings, Varuna's umbrella and the peak of mount Mandara. Bhumi Devi requested Lord Krishna to install Bhagadatta, as the new king of Pragjyotishpuram. Bhagadatta was the son of Narakasura. Lord Krishna freed the royal maidens, whom Bhauma had kidnapped from various kingdoms. To restore their honor, he married all the sixteen thousand princesses, and then sent them in palanquins to Dwaraka.

On the following day, which happened to be the Amavasya or New Moon day. The Goddess Bhumi declared the removal of the ban. All the people of Pragjyotishpuram allowed to light the lamps in their houses as well as in the streets. The day on which Narakasura died was the Chaturdashi of Kartika Masam. That's why it's called as 'Naraka Chaturdashi'. Since then, it has become a tradition for the people of India to celebrate Deepavali. The festival of lights falls on the new moon day of Kartika Masam as per the Lunar Calendar of Hindus. The Diwali Celebrations also coincide with the day on which Lord Rama and Sita return to Ayodhya.

Symbolism of Naraka Chaturdashi

The Shrimad Bhagavata has the following description to describe the misdeeds of the demon Narakasura:

"**Narakasura, the son of Dharitri, the earth, tried to grasp the whole sky, and for this he was killed by the Lord in a fight.**"

Based on the above description, the Narakasura story nothing but the TOBA volcanic eruption. In those days, the impact might be visible as far as the Mandara mountain. The volcanic eruption occurs due to a fissure on Earth's inner crust. The magma and gases belong the interior of the Earth (Dharitri). They exploit the weak zones in the lithosphere to reach the surface. The Puranic Rishis called this eruption as the son of the Dharitri. The ash erupted from vent of volcano become ash clouds. It can travel vast distances from the crater. The volcanic ash falls across wide areas blocking the whole night sky. The Rishis interpreted this as the son of Earth, Narakasura, grasping the whole sky. The Shrimad Bhagavata defines the fortifications of Pragjyotishpuram as follows:

"**Pragyotisa-pura, which as surrounded on all sides by the fortifications consists of hills, unmanned weapons, water, fire and wind** ..."

It's known since ancient times; the volcanic activity could result into violent explosions. When it reaches the earth surface from which ash, stream, gases, and molten rocks erupt into air. The lava or the molten magma harmful to the humans. Which the Sages interpreted as the fortifications. Most of the Bhagavata stories are fictitious. The Rishis created this type of Romantic stories to promote the Lord Krishna Avatar. This Narakasura story was in existence for long time even before the time of Lord Krishna. This shows that the cultural continuity happening in India for more than eighty thousand years.

14. Adolf Hitler – An Aryan Dictator

"I swore never to be silent whenever and wherever human beings endure suffering and humiliation. We must always take sides. Neutrality helps the oppressor, never the victim. Silence encourages the tormentor, never the tormented."

-Elie Wiesel

Chronology (all dates CE)

April 20, 1889	Hitler born in Braunau am Inn, Austria-Hungary border town
1914 -1918	First world war started for silly reasons such as spirited nationalism in Europe; 32 nations took part.
1920	Hitler joined the Nazi Party (National Socialist German Worker's Party)
1921	Hitler becomes the Führer of Nazi party
1933	Austrian born Hitler without any formal education becomes the Chancellor of Germany; Hitler and his collaborators instituted euthanasia (mercy killing) and sterilization to install their idea of Aryan racial purity.
1938	Kristallnacht (Night of Broken Glass); 30,000 Jews sent to concentration camps
1939	Beginning of World War II
1940	France, Netherlands and Belgium fell to Germany
1941	"Operation Barbarossa", German Tanks advances towards Soviet border
1941	Hitler stops euthanasia based on the public uproar.
May, 1942	Subhas Chandra Bose meets Hitler and agrees to the conditions set by Nazis.
July, 1942	Bose, openly criticizes Hitler attempt to invade Soviet Union and decides to leave for Japan
April, 1943	Mass grave found in Katyn, Poland; Nazis held responsible for atrocities.
June 6, 1944	Normandy beach, D-Day invasion. Total 176,000 troops of America, Great Britain and Canada

	involved. The largest seaborne invasion in the Modern human history
June, 1944	Germans unleashed V1 pilotless flying bomber **(First Drone known to the modern world history)**
Aug, 1944	Germany soldiers in Paris surrender to allied forces
April, 1945	Soviet tankers enter Berlin
April 30, 1945	Hitler marries his lover Eva Braun before committing suicide
8 May, 1945	V-day, Germany surrenders to Soviet & Allied forces

Who was Hitler?

Adolf Hitler was one of the most dreadful military leaders and the powerful dictators of the 20th century. Hitler transformed the FDR (Federal Republic of Germany) from the state of virtual bankruptcy to one of the greatest militarized societies of the modern human history with in a span of less than 5 years. Hitler believed that the Aryans (in this case native Germans and Austrians) were the superior race. And he also thought they deserved more than they had. More amenities such as Lebensraum (living space), higher standard of living etc. Hitler targeted Jews and other races in the name of Aryan Superiority and Lebensraum.

In 1920, Hitler formed the National Socialist German Worker's Party. It's called as NAZI and adopted the Swastika as the party symbol. The Swastika was the popular Vedic symbol in India during the 2nd century BCE. During the late 1930s, the Hitler's team visited the Vedic Rishis in India and Tibet to find out the details about the nuclear and chemical weapons used in the Mahabharata war. Based on the inscriptions, the astronomical calculations and archeological findings the Mahabharata war occurred 5000 years ago, the war happened in the year 3138 BCE at a place called Kurukshetra, Northern India. Around two million people and one million animals (horses & elephants) killed in the war. More than one million people died on the last day, the 18th day of the war. It was due to the impact of the ancient nuclear and chemical weapons (known as Divya Astra).

How an Austrian tramp (Homeless person) could become the Chancellor of Germany?

Hitler was born in 1889, in Braunau am Inn, Austria-Hungary border town to Klara and Alios Hitler. Hitler's father worked in the Austrian custom service. Because of his father's influence, Hitler had above average grades at the schools. Hitler father wanted him to enter civil service after the school. But Hitler decided to join Realschule, a secondary school that prepares students for higher education in language arts and technology. During his time at Realschule, Hitler began to form his political views. It was the beginning of his views on German nationalism and anti-Semitism. Hitler's father passed away in January 1903, because of this Hitler became the sole bread winner for the family. In October 1907, Hitler went to Vienna with an intention to join the Vienna Academy of fine Arts & Architecture, but the school didn't admit him. After his mother died in 1908, Hitler continued to stay at Vienna, with a pretext of studies to collect the Orphan's pension. Finally, Hitler moved to a homeless shelter after all his funds were exhausted.

While staying at the homeless shelter, Hitler exposed to the extreme political ideology, mostly to the lectures of Lanz von Liebenfels. Per Liebenfels publications Aryans are the superior race, and Jews and all other races are inferior. In 1913, at the age of 25, Hitler moved from Vienna to Munich, with an intention to make his living by selling paintings and drawing pictures on public buildings. In January 1914, Austrian Military summoned Hitler for services. But, later they excused him form the services as he couldn't pass the medical fitness test.

The outbreak of World War I, in August 1914, was a major advantage for Hitler. He volunteered for a 16th Bavarian regiment unit in the Germany. Known as LIST Regiment, named after the founder. Hitler volunteered for a dangerous role, the regimental message runner. The German military refused to promote him because of his Austrian ethnicity, which they thought an inferior race to lead Germans. And hence Hitler remained in the rank of Corporal (ranking next below a sergeant). In 1914, Hitler won the 'Iron cross second class' and later, in April 1918. Hitler got an award of 'Iron cross first class', for a bravery of capturing an enemy officer and a dozen enemy soldiers. Hitler was in the same regiment where Lieutenant Wiedemann and Sergeant Max Amann, both of whom would become the prominent members of Hitler's Nazi party at the later stage.

In October 1918, while fighting near Ypres, Hitler suffered temporary blindness. It happened due to the mustard gas attack. He was sent to a hospital in Pasewalk, Eastern Germany. After the discharge from the hospital, posted back to Munich barracks. The first World War ended on November 11, 1918 before he reached Munich. And the whole Germany was in an utter chaos. In September 1919, Hitler was part of the army intelligence. He was sent to investigate the German Worker's party (or DAP, later became Nazi party). One of the many nationalist, anti-semantic racist groups showed up in postwar years. Hitler joined the Nazi Party (National Socialist German Worker's Party) in 1920, because the anti-sematic and racist party ideology appealed to him. And his talent in public speaking drew huge crowds and he later become the spokesperson. By the year 1923, aftermath of the World War I, the German was facing with massive inflation. And growing civil unrest, at this point Hitler decided the time was right for the revolution.

On November 8, 1923, Hitler and his 600 members of SA took Gustav von Kahr as the hostage in a Munich beer hall. The SA stands for Sturmabteilung, a paramilitary wing of Nazi party. Gustav von Kahr was the head of the provincial Bavarian government. The revolt failed next day after the police shot down 16 of the Hitler's followers. The police arrested Hitler. After the trial, he sentenced to five years in prison for treason and later released after one year. Even though putsch (revolt) failed it was an important lesson for Hitler:

"To destroy the democracy of any country never fight as an outsider. But by working within the system and avoid confrontation with Military, Police powers and Media."

While in the prison, he dictated the first volume of Mein Kampf. It means "My struggle", it was translated in 1939. And after the release within one year he completed the second volume. Hitler believed the superior Aryan race centered in Germany, would rule the world. Hitler denounced the political parties as **stupid political parties**. He wanted to reverse the 1919 "Treaty of Versailles" and reclaim what Germany had lost because of the bad agreements. The Treaty of Versailles (Peace Treaty), signed on June 28, 1919. It was between German and the allied forces. This treaty forced Germany to disarm, to give up territorial authority and to accept the responsibility for all the war damages. Hitler thought it was a stupid deal. The Treaty also forced Germany to pay excessive amount of reparations, because of this treaty certain allied countries benefited a lot. Many historians considered this too harsh. Another major idea was about Lebensraum (living space). Hitler argued that the Germany needed large amounts of territory. Hitler thought conquering more territory was the solution. Based on another idea floating around, he wanted to either kill or expel the inferior non-Aryan locals.

Upon his release from Jail in December 1924, he built up a network of local party organizations (SA). And organized the black-shirted defense crop Schutzstaffel called "SS". The role of SS was to protect him and as well as take control of the party. Hitler decided to build the party by democratic means. His Nazi party received just under 3% votes in the 1928 elections. But during the campaign the party gained a strong base. In late 1929, there was a major economic depression in America. The effects of this Great depression could be felt as far as in Europe and Germany. Because of this economic crisis, the Weimar Republic fell in March, 1930. This was another huge opportunity for Hitler. In the new elections held in the September that year, the Nazis won with overwhelming votes. They won 107 representatives in Reichstag (German Parliament), a jump from previous count of 12. The rise of nationalist Nazi majority caused the foreign investors to withdraw money from Germany, which resulted in the collapse of the German Banking system. The unemployment rose and people lost faith in other parties. Whereas Hitler and his Nazi colleagues were effective in offering simplistic but appealing solutions to the country's problems.

In elections held in 1932, the Nazis received more votes than any other party. After the landslide victory, Hitler demanded President Hindenburg to appoint him as the chancellor. On January 30, 1933, Hitler was sworn in as the Chancellor of Germany. Immediately after that he was successful in persuading the President Hindenburg to issue a decree suspending all civil liberties. Hitler could convince him to pass the **'enabling act'**. Which authorized Hitler government to make laws without any legislative approval. That was the beginning of the world's most notorious totalitarian regime in Germany.

Bose meets Hitler to free India

Subhas Chandra Bose, the commander-in-chief of "Azad-e-Hindu force", considered as the "Hero of India" for his efforts to free India from British crown. Bose planned the Military attack from outside India. Which was a direct contrast to the Mahatma Gandhi's doctrine of non-violence. In January 1941, Bose escaped from the house arrest in West Bengal, India. And then flew to Berlin with help of Russian military. In May, 1941 meets Himmler and convinces him about his plan to free India with the help of POW and trained Indian forces.

Illustration 14.1: Bose meets Hitler in May, 1942 to discuss about Azad legion (free India) military

Bose finally meets Hitler for the first time in September 1941. He proposed an agreement with Hitler, according to this Germany should recognize India as a free country and in return for rebellion against the British. Hitler didn't accept Bose's plan of freeing India with the help of Indian POWs. Because he was pursuing a secret pact with Briton through some unidentified channels. Hitler wanted to conquer the world based on both German and Briton superior Aryan races, and they should rule the world.

The war dynamics changed with Japan attacking Pearl harbor in December 1941. And immediately after that United States declared war. In January 1942, Germany stalls military action and help needed to free India. Instead agrees to establish a radio broadcast station for Bose to address Indians around the world from Germany. In February 1942, many Indian POWs captured in Singapore by the Japanese forces. In May, 1942 Bose meets Hitler again (as shown in the illustration 14.1) and agrees to the Hitler's proposal. Based on this Bose reports to Hitler and gets arms in return. Hitler declares Bose as the leader of India on a condition that it gets independence after the end of war[1].

In July 1942, Bose gets disillusioned with Hitler and German plans to invade Soviet. Bose was the first person to recognize that fighting with Soviet Union was a suicidal step by Hitler. He expresses displeasure and initiates contact with Japanese. In August 1942, Bose and his advisors drew up the plans for establishment of INA (Indian national Army) with the help of Japan, and Bose decided to leave Germany. Even though Bose was openly critical of Hitler's plans of invasion of Soviet Union, Hitler concurs with Bose's proposal of getting Japanese help instead of Germany. As a gesture of Good will, Hitler provided Three tons of gold bricks to establish initial army, and the submarine to avoid any aerial attacks by the allied forces. In December 1942, Bose leaves Germany in the Nazi submarine (U-180). And, disembarks at Madagascar and boards the Japanese submarine (I-29) in January, 1943. In March, 1944, with the help of 40,000 INA troops, Subash Chandra Bose staged a military campaign against British on Indo-Burma frontier. The military complain of Indian National Army continued until August, 1945 with some minor success in North East India, and they were forced to retreat the same year following the Japanese surrender. On August 17, 1945, the plane in which Bose was a passenger suddenly disappeared from the radar while fleeing from Singapore to Japan. According to the Japanese News Agency, Bose had died in a plane crash in Taihoku (Taiwan) on August 18, 1945.

Gestapo

In April 1933, Hermman Göring founded Gestapo (Geheime Staatspolizei). He was one of the Adolf Hitler's lieutenants. The Gestapo was nothing but a state sponsored secret police. It worked with SD (security service), to persecute political opponents of Nazi party. A decree in February, 1933 removed the constitutional protection against arbitrary arrest. It was at Gestapo's direction the political suspects were arrested and sent to concentration camps. The Jews, Roma (Gypsies), homosexuals, and other religious dissidents put in the concentration camps.

During the 1930s six major camps established. There were located at Dachau, Buchenwald, Saschsenhausen, Flossenburg, Mauthausen and Raensbruck. Each camp held about 25,000 prisoners in 1939. During the World War II the Nazi leaders established 22 camps and increased the camp size. Many prisoners worked to death in chemical and rocket factories. The inmates became the guinea pigs for medical experiments. The Nazis killed those who were not able to work. By various means such as by lethal injections, shooting or gassing etc.

Holocaust

In 1933, Hitler and his collaborators instituted euthanasia, another name for mercy killing. Nazi Germany also passed "Forced Sterilization" law to install their idea of Aryan racial purity. According to some unverified sources, in January 1934, as many as 4 million people were sterilized. Between 1933 to 1945, they killed anywhere from 9 million to 17 million non-Aryan people, out of which 6 million were Jews. No evidence found to confirm the death of 17 million people. Some humanitarian agencies confirmed the death toll in thousands instead of Millions. They attributed this to the allied bombings on the concentration camps. Some agencies claimed the total population of Jews in Europe actually increased a little bit after the World War II as compared to the pre-war estimates (no way to confirm if its Fake news or not). In spite of pro-Nazi propaganda, the death toll was estimated based on the circumstantial evidence. Such as medical records, letters to family members, a talk in the local bars about the gas chambers and SS execution squads, etc. During the World War II, the Nazis also established several extermination camps, with an intention to eradicate entire Jews population.

Illustration 14.2: Concentration camps during the holocaust era (1943- 1944)

In January 1942, Adolf Eichmann, organized the "Final Solution". He was the head of the Gestapo's "Jews Evacuation Department". Per which all the Jews should be eliminated. The mass deportation was ruled out as an impractical solution, because of the ongoing World War -II. Directives were sent to move the Jews towards East as part of the "territorial solution".

Per Christopher Ailsby (author of a book on third Reich):

"At no point killing was mentioned, recipients were expected to understand the meaning of "FINAL solution", "deportation to East". The policy of extermination went forward until the end of war. Accurate numbers are impossible to get, but estimates run as high as 15 million, including 6 million Jews. They were liquidated in the camps or by mass executions in isolated places"

As per the United States Holocaust Memorial Museum, the concentration camps have become the most powerful symbols of the Holocaust. The SS (black-shirted Schutzstaffel) established "extra camps", 22 "main camps" and more than 1100 affiliated sub camps. Himmer was responsible for the massive increase in the sub-camps during the World War - II period (Illustration 14.2).

During the World War II, several repressive regimes have established the concentration camps. Soviet Union put as many as 15 million dissidents in the Bolsheviks labor camps. Many of these inmates were released after the death of Soviet Communist leader, Joseph Stalin in 1953. According to the western scholars, Stalin joins the list of the most brutal dictators of 20th century. Stalin launched major campaigns of Industrialization and Political terror, millions of people were arrested and deported to labor camps. Soviet historians contradicted this and they claimed Stalin regime as the Great one. It is indisputable, Stalin was the most powerful person of the 20th Century. He personally directed war against Nazi Germany and defeated them in the battle of Stalingrad, during 1942 -1943.

Illustration 14.3: U.S. Troops wading through massive Nazi gunfire on D-day

D-Day

On June 6, 1944, D-Day, the allied forces launched operation overload. The countries involved in this operation were United States, Briton, and Canada. It was under the supreme command of the United States General Dwight Eisenhower, the allied forces landed on the Normandy beaches. That was the beginning of the end of the "Third Reich". The allied landing involving more than 150,00 troops. With the support of 5000 naval vessels and 11,000 planes. The American troops landed on the two beaches.

In the west side of Normandy, France codenamed "Omaha" and "Utah". British and Canadian troops landed on the five beaches on the east side. The allied forces suffered heavy causalities, around 14,000 (Illustration 14.3). The Normandy campaign ended on August 19, 1944.

with capture of 50, 000 German soldiers. The Allies were now able to advance swiftly across the northern France and Belgium. And finally reached the borders of Netherlands in early September, 1944 [2].

End of Hitler's Regime

Hitler had clearly undermined the resilience of the Soviet Union troops in fighting back. Germans had come so close to capturing Moscow. But not quite well in breaking the soviet defense lines. And they were finally thrown out of soviet territory. The things also didn't go well in North Africa. Rommel (German field marshal, 1891-1944) didn't get enough support from Hitler. He had been not allowed to get enough supplies and troops as the results of a war with Soviet Union. Because of this being forced out of Africa in March 1943 before the complete surrender of Afrika Korps. The German Military finally lost confidence in Hitler. Between March 1943 and July 1944, several assassination attempts carried out to kill Hitler. But, none of these attempts succeeded. The biggest mistake Hitler ever made was underestimating Americans, in December 1944. He launched last German offensive against the Allied armies. He sent his last remaining reserves towards west in to the Ardennes county of Belgium and Luxembourg. This German's suicidal offensive called as "Battle of Bulge". It took place between December 1944 and January 1945. And more than 2,40,000 German soldiers lost their lives.

Since the troops much needed in the east were sent to west to fight the allied forces. The soviet troops and tankers didn't find any resistance in entering Berlin. It was Germany's final humiliation, when the Soviet troops captured Reichstag (German Parliament Building) on April 30, 1945. Per the historians, on the same day Hitler married his lover and mistress Eva Braun. The ceremony presumably took place in his bunker and shortly after that both committed suicide. On May 8, 1945, V-day,

Germany surrendered to the allies, marking the end of Nazi regime that was responsible for death of millions of people. The historians estimated around Eighty million people died worldwide during the world war-II, out of which Six million Jews and Seven million Indians (Sikhs, Gurkhas, Nepalese, and other missing people) and 20 million Soviet troops. There were different versions of stories floating around about the war causalities, and it's hard to find out which one to believe. Because some of the missing people might have actually survived and migrated to other parts of the world.

Section - IV

(Yoga, Meditation & Shiva Thandavam)

15. Bhakti Yoga & Meditation

"The unending endeavour to bridge the gap between the finite and the infinite is mysticism"

(Shrii Shrii Anandamurti)

What is AM Bhakti Yoga?

Quite surprisingly the AM (Ananda Marga) Bhakti yoga methods are far more effective than the TM (Transcendental meditation). There are several cases where people followed TM for twenty plus years with absolutely no improvement, whereas the AM meditation showed results in less than two months. This sounds like too good to be true, but there are real world cases available to substantiate this. The point I am trying to make here is, just by sitting in the Meditation pose doesn't take you anywhere. Let us not forget, AM Yoga means not just practicing a Asana, it's a philosophy, a combination of Niyamas (purification methods), Breathing Techniques, Asana and Meditation. The Yoga instructors of AM (Guru) will teach you the best Yoga and Meditation techniques designed to achieve the optimum results.

Several years ago, I went to Middle East on a business trip. One of my colleagues gave me a ride from Haifa to Jerusalem. During the trip, he told me that the Yoga and Meditation doesn't work. I was surprised; how could the time-tested methods go wrong? I immediately asked him what type of meditation you do and how long? It appeared to be Transcendental Meditation (TM) and 30 minutes every morning. I heard several complaints about TM, it may not be true that the meditation doesn't work. But the expectations are too high. The people have no patience to wait for twenty years, they want quick results.

AM Meditation Process

The AM meditation technique is always custom designed to suit the induvial needs, because the technique that works for one person may not be effective for another person. The AM meditation process consists of three stages as revealed by the Shri Acharya Savitananda, Global

Illustration 15.1: Shri Acharya Savitananda, Head of Global Meditation and Bhakti Yoga and also Principal of Ananda Marga Group of Schools for Young Children, delivering the sermon on Bhakti Yoga at Hyderabad, Telangana, India.

A brief History of Shri Acharya Savitanandaji

Ac. Savitanandaji was a Gold Medalist and Graduate student of Gandhi Medical College, Hyderabad and spent several decades in Europe, Asia & Africa in Humanitarian and Flood relief operations wing of Ananda Marga, the United Nations Non-Governmental Agency.

Head for Meditation and Bhakti Yoga and also Principal of Ananda Marga Group of Schools for Young Children, Hyderabad, Telangana, India. The AM meditation process consists of three stages

1. Yama and Niyama
2. Kirtan Dance (5 to 15 Minutes, Shiva Thandavam or Kaoshiki Dance)
3. Meditation (5 to 15 Minutes)

AM - Moralism

There are Ten moral principles one need to follow before beginning the AM Yoga & Meditation, these are called as YAMA and NIYAMA. Apart from Yama and Niyama, there are set of Mantras and weekly group meditation programs (called as Dharmacakra) to improve the overall meditation experience, please contact the Yoga instructor of any nearest Ananda Marga ashram for more details.

YAMA

Yama contains 5 sets of moral principles:

- Ahimsa – Not to harm anybody
- Satya – Benevolent truthfulness
- Asteya – Not to steal anybody's property
- Brahmacharya – It means Brahma (God) is in all expressions of Universe. This doesn't mean remain unmarried, but expects you to follow the moral values.
- Aparigraha – To keep the low carbon footage and keep the world green, follow simple living style and avoid unnecessary luxuries.

NIYAMA

Niyama consisting of five moral principles one should always follow:

- SHAOCA – Insists on Internal and External purity and cleanliness
- SANTOSHA – Importance of Contentment, Satisfaction and Mental Equilibrium
- TAPAH – Selfless service
- SHADHVAVA – Keeping uplifting company, group meditation once a week and reading spiritual books
- ISHVARA PRANIDHANA – Meditate that you are an inseparable part of Supreme Consciousness (BABA)

AM - Kirtan Dance

Hold the hands together at the level of the heart or keep raised above the head as shown in the Illustration 15.2. Alternately step by tapping the big toe of one foot behind the heel of the other foot while bending the knees. Touching the toe in this manner triggers a reaction in the Pineal gland at the top of the head, causing mind to relax. While performing the dance, you may sing the mantra "BABA NAM KEVALAM" (meaning Supreme Consciousness all there is) while mind concentrated at the top of the head, the Sahasrara Cakra, one of the seven Cakras located along the body axis. The other chakras located at perineum, genitals, solar plexus, heart, throat, and between eyes. The steps for performing the Kaoshiki dance while singing the 'BABA NAM KEV ALAM" mantra is given in the illustration 15.3.

Illustration 15.2: Shiva Thandavam Dance (courtesy Acharya
Savitananda; head of Global Meditation, Ananda Marga)

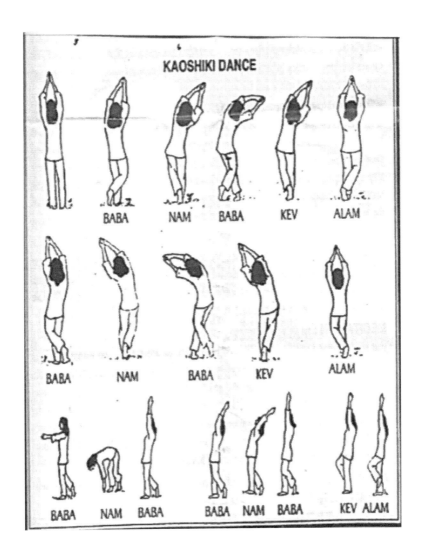

Illustration 15.3: Kaoshiki Dance (courtesy Shri Acharya Savitananda; head of Global Meditation, Ananda Marga)

AM Meditation Method

Sit in a cross legged position (Padmashana pose) on the flat floor with right feet above the left feet. Close your eyes and think in your mind that the Supreme Consciousness (BABA) is all there all around you and within you. You are one with that. While you are ideating on this feeling repeat 'BABA NAM' as you breathe in and 'KEVALAM' as your breath out. The instructor of AM might fine tune and tell you what to do while breath-in and breath-out and its different for each person. Practice this for at least fifteen minutes twice a day to achieve best results such as improved concentration and memory power. By the way, never ever use any alarm clocks to determine the time, let your internal biological clock decide this.

Exercise (Optional):

Here is a 2-step scientific method to prove that the AM method really works:

1) Take the CT scan of your brain before starting the meditation process.

2) Perform AM Meditation twice a day for Six months and then take another CT scan of your brain and compare two CT scan reports for any differences. There should be a distinguishable improvement in the Cingulate Cortex, which lies above the Corpus Callosum (neural fiber beneath the cortex) that connects the Frontal lobe and the Temporal lobe.

16. Yoga Philosophy

"He who perceives inaction in action and action in inaction, has among men attained real knowledge; even while performing all action, he is doing yoga"

-Bhagavad Gita (IV-18), translated by C. Rajagopalachari

(The Great Teacher of Yoga, King of mythical city Dwaraka Lord Krishna gives a sermon on Karma Yoga to the Pandavas Prince Arjuna on the 250-kilometer-long battle site of Kurukshetra war; in the year 3138 BCE)

Chronology

4000 BCE- 3000 BCE	Yoga Terracotta - archeological evidence found in the Indus Valley excavations (Proto-Shiva in Yoga pose most probably Shiva's son Skanda).
3138 BCE	Lord Krishna delivered sermon on Karma Yoga (Bhagvad Gita) to Pandavas Prince Arujuna on the battle field of Kurukshetra. Bhagvad Gita refers to the philosophies of Yoga Sastra and Samkhya Shastra.
1500 BCE	Advaita Vedanta (Adi Shankara's Hindu Philosophy) introduces Yoga Sutras for the first time to the common people.
1000 BCE	Murugan Shiva's son becomes popular deity in South India (source: Tolkappiyam)
400BCE- 200 BCE	Sage Patanjali introduces "Yoga sutras of Patanjali" – 196 sutras, mostly extracted from the ancient Yogic traditions. Due to the errors made by ancient historians as they identified wrong persons with Patanjali, it's hard to find out the exact date. So, Sage Patanjali might have lived between 4th century BCE and 2nd Century BCE.

What is Yoga?

Sage Patanjali introduced "Yoga sutras of Patanjali", 196 sutras, mostly extracted from the old puranic traditions sometime between fourth century BCE (400 BC) and second century BCE (200 BC). Pretty much all the ancient Indian scriptures, Vedas, Agamas, Puranas, Itihāsas, and Dharma Shāstras have references to some form of Yoga. Yoga is the object of knowledge or technique of realization through combination of consciousness and unconsciousness mind.

S. No.	Methods of Yoga	Definition
1	Hatha Yoga	Identification through Strength, or through the sun-moon conjunction.
2	Raja Yoga	Identification through Royal way of integration. ‡
3	Mantra Yoga	By means of hermetic utterances.
4	Laya Yoga (Kundalini)	Identification by mergence.
5	Shiva Yoga	Yoga through Devotion and Metaphysical principle.
6	Jnāna Yoga	Yoga through Knowledge.
7	Tantra Yoga	Yoga through Tantric methods or rules of Terrestrial knowledge.
8	Karma Yoga	Re-integration or identification of body and mind through actions.

Table 16.1: Various methods of Yoga

‡ The Hatha Yoga is the preparation or prerequisite to the Raja Yoga.

In other words, Yoga is the key to uncover the ancient Indian philosophy explained in Upanishads, Puranas, Agamas, Gita etc. The word Yoga means 'that which unites' or 'links together'. According to Veda Vyasa (author of Mahabharata) it's a re-integration or identification of body and mind through two kinds of states - consciousness mind and unconsciousness one. There are various methods of Yoga[1] (as shown in the table 16.1) and each method has eight steps. The regular people are advised to follow the first five steps or up to seventh step. The Eighth step is meant for the advanced Yogis or the people who dedicated their life to Spirituality (dissolution of individual being into the total being). According to the Vedanta, the goal of Yogi is the supreme realization, the main obstacle of realization is the constant activity of mind. But there are intermediate stages towards reunion of oneself with Supreme Self, can also be called as Yoga.

Definition of Hatha Yoga

Hatha Yoga (syllable '**Ha**' means Sun and syllable '**tha**' -- Moon) means conjunction (yoga) of the sun and moon. The practice through which body and vital energies can be brought under control. Yogi achieves his/her aim by coordinating the most powerful vital impulses   Prana (respiratory) and Apana (digestive). The Hatha Yoga is the basic form of a Yoga and it's a preparation and prerequisite to the Raja Yoga or Laya Yoga (Kundalini Yoga). If your goal is to get the cure for alignments such as Chronic Fatigue, Insomnia, Stomach disorders, Chronic Headaches, Diabetes, Spine problems etc. Then practicing Raja Yoga is the solution, but you need to start with basic Yoga and Meditation explained in this chapter.

The great exponent of Ancient Indian Yoga, Sage Patanjali explained the Astanga, the eight limbs of Yoga. The eight main steps of Hatha Yoga are listed below:
1) Abstinence
2) Observances (Niyama)

3) Sitting postures

4) breath control

5) Withdrawal of mind from external objects

6) Concentration

7) Contemplation and identification

8) Identification with Supreme Reality

Based on the descriptions in the Goraksha Samihitā, the last four steps are called Antara-Anga (Inner Stage) and the first four steps are Bhira-anga (Outer Stage). The purification of Inner Stage (first four steps) is compulsory for all. The regular people may practice the steps five through seven and the 8th step is mainly for the Sadhus or people who practice extreme asceticism in order to achieve mystic liberation or super human powers. As per Indian nationalist and Mystic Philosopher Sri Aurobindo Ghose (born August 15, 1872):

"Salvation involves a two-way path; the Enlightenment comes from the divinity above, but all the human beings possess a spiritual "supermind" that enables them to reach upward illumination. The ultimate fusion of divinity and the supermind leads to spiritual perfection, which can be achieved through practice of Yoga. "

Abstinence: The First Step of Hatha Yoga

Patanjali explained in Yoga Darshana (2-30) the list of abstinences as Satya, Ahimsā, Asteya, Aparigraha and Brahmacharya. The abstinences are important and essential step in bringing the body and mind to the highest possible efficiency.

1. **Satya** (meaning Truth): It's very difficult to explain the definition of Truth in this modern age of Fake information. The testimony of inner consent without any deceit and with

an aim of doing good and in friendly words is considered Truth.

2. **Ahimsa** (meaning Nonviolence): As per Patanjali, all observations lead up to Ahimsa, one has to bring all other abstinences in to action before Ahimsa can be attained. It's the policy of restraining from use of force when reacting against discrimination, oppression or injustice. A person is not ready for Hatha Yoga unless and until practice abstinence from causing bodily or mental pain to anyone including oneself, however small it is.

3. **Asteya** (meaning Non-stealing): Not to take away another person's belongings or ideas without an intention to return or acknowledge. According to Veda Vyāsa acceptance by Yogi any amount of gift money or any kind of wealth not permitted by the Vedic Scriptures is considered Stealing.

4. **Aparigraha** (meaning Non-possession): The possession of any means of enjoyment with depriving others leads to violence and attachment and hence it must be restrained by the persons willing to practice Hatha Yoga.

5. **Brahmacharya** (meaning Chastity or avoid extra-marital relationship): Refraining from the perturbation and emotions either in mind or body is considered chastity. As explained in Brahmanas and Daksha Samhitā: to think about it, to talk or joke about it, to praise about it, to look with an intention or desire, to make conversation in private, to decide, to attempt or actually doing it is considered erotic actions. One should avoid such as actions in order to optimize body and mind.

Table 16.2: Various methods of Yoga snāna

Type of Bath	Type of snāna	Description
Celestial	Divya	Taking bath in rain while looking at Sun
Watery	Vārunya	Immersion in a river
Air	Vāyavya	Immersed in a dust
Fiery	Āgneya	Immersion in ashes
Earthly	Bhauma	Wrapped in a cloth
Rune	Mantra	Ritual bath with Hermetic utterances
Mental	Mānasa	Immersion of mind in Divine Contemplation

Niyama: Second Step of Hatha Yoga

The Upanishads talk about additional five observations or Niyamas, these are Forgiveness, Purity, Endurance, Rectitude (moral virtue) and Temperance (to avoid too much Alcohol or Food).

Purity: When we talk about purity, there are two kinds - inward purity and outward purity. Purity is an essential part of all the Yoga methods but it has a different priority based on which method you follow. For example, in Mantra Yoga it means to act selflessly and that's what is given greater importance.

Outward Purity: The outward purity obtained through eating pure food, to cleanse one's own body through bathing, etc.

Purity of Place achieved by sitting under one of the sacred trees such as Pippal, Banian, Ashoka tree, etc. Purity of direction obtained through facing East or North. There are seven types of actions or bathing (snāna) used to obtain Bodily purity (Table 16.2). The Mental bath and Mantra snāna are considered immersion of mind in Divine or ritual bath.

Inward purity: Its achieved through control over the senses, Charity, Friendship, Kindness, ritual sacrifices, truth, endurance, forgiveness, Non-violence, Simplicity and abstaining from Greed, Enmity, Anger, Agitation, I-assertion, possessiveness, Attachment, etc.

Āsana: Third Step of Hatha Yoga

According to Yoga Darshana, Āsanas or sitting postures are essential to strengthen the physical body and stabilize the mind. Theoretically speaking, as many as Eighty-four thousand postures are possible in Yoga. But, the most basic posture Padma-Āsana or Lotus posture is good enough for the beginners of Hatha Yoga. The Hatha Yoga is the first stage in Yoga practice, the Raja Yoga and Kundalini Yoga may require more postures (as many as 84 Āsanas) and which should be learned under the supervision of Guru (Yoga Teacher).

Padma-Āsana or Lotus posture: Sit on the floor with Left foot placed on the Right thigh and Right foot placed on the Left thigh, the arms can be either placed on the knees as shown in Illustration **16.1** or go around the back and catch hold of the toes. The Shiva Samhitā suggests – the tongue should touch the teeth root, press the chin against the chest, and eyes should be focused on the tip of the nose.

Illustration 16.1: Goutham Buddha in Lotus posture, 1th century BCE, Sarnath, India (©ASI)

Illustration 16.2 Maha Yogi Shiva in yoga (attainment) pose, who introduced yoga to the world
(Monolithic 16th Rock cave built by Rastrakutas in 8th Century CE, Ellora caves, India ©ASI)

The Padma-Āsana is the best Āsana recommended for everyone as this posture cures Heart disease, Lung disease, Fever, Skin problems and Digestive troubles etc. This posture awakes the coiled energy (Kundalini), so after performing this Āsana immediate walking should be avoided. If practicing Padma-Āsana is difficult for you, then you may practice the posture of attainment (Illustration 16.2) until your body flexible enough to do Padma-Āsana. But this pose of attainment has some side effects, it may weaken male organ and should not be practiced by married men. Padma-Āsana posture doesn't have any side effects and it can be practiced by anyone.

Table 16.3: Some common Hatha Yoga & Raja Yoga Postures and Benefits

Sanskrit Name (Āsana)	English name (posture)	Cure for the Diseases/Disorders
Bhadra	Cow-Keeping	Digestive problem
Supta-Vajrasana	Supine Firm	Pelvis and muscle toning
Mukta	Liberated	Root contraction
Simha	Lion	Muscular contraction
Shirsha	Head	Spine
Anjanaya	Salutation	Concentration and improve balance
Ardha-matsyendra	Half-Spinal	Back Pain, Sex problems and Constipation
Bhujangasana	Cobra	Spine problems
Sasamgasana	Hare	Headache
Vrikasana	Tree	Centering & Right Posture
Parvatasana	The Mountain	Lungs & Diaphragm
Chakrasana (not recommended for women)	Circle	Antidote to Obesity
Uddiyana	Stomach lift	Liver & Stomach disorders
Vajrasana	Firm	Attaining Stability of Mind
Garudasana	The Twisted	Good for Arms & Legs

Note: If you are new to yoga, never attempt yoga posture alone; find a qualified Yoga Guru instead. Yoga cures chronic diseases in a long run; for immediate medical attention visit the medical physician instead.

Prānāyāma: Fourth Step of Hatha Yoga

Breathing is one of the most important techniques of yoga. According to Yoga Darshana (2.49), the voluntary action of breathing in (prāna) and breathing out (apāna) is called Prānāyāma.

Table 16.4: Various methods of breath-in, breath-out and holding breath

Breathing Method	Breathing Technique	Breath-in (Seconds)	Holding breath (Seconds)	Breath-out (Seconds)
Outward Chalice	Breath out first, hold breath then Breath-in	5	16	5
Inward Chalice	Breath in first, hold breath and Breath-out	5	16	5
Absolute Chalice	Breath in first, hold breath and Breath-out	5	16	8
Small Chalice	Breath in first, hold breath and Breath-out	4	16	8
Intermediate Chalice	Breath in first, hold breath and Breath-out	6	32	12
Higher Chalice	Breath in first, hold breath and Breath-out	8	50	16

If you are new to yoga first start with basic steps and then gradually increase it. When you are sitting in a Lotus (**Padma-Āsana**) posture close the right nose with left hand, belly is drawn in and breath in through left nose for 5 Seconds and then hold the breadth and belly for another 5 seconds, after that restore the belly to normal position and exhale for 5 seconds.   While holding the breadth keep still and don't move any body parts. This process of holding breath while standstill is called as Kumbhaka (Chalice).   Repeat the same steps with left nose closed. Try at least twenty breath-in & breath-outs, two times a day, before moving onto the more advanced Prānāyāma steps as shown in the table 16.4.

Pratyāhāra: Fifth Step of Hatha Yoga

Withdrawal of mind from external objects (Pratyāhāra) is the method of detangling the senses from the objects of its natural perception. No one can become Yogi without renouncing the desires and control the senses. The main method of achieving the Withdrawal is by practicing the "Absolute Chalice".   Take the Lotus posture and breath-in for 5 seconds and then stop all the motion of breath for 16 seconds or 32 seconds. Then breath out for 8 seconds and repeat the Absolute Chalice" as shown in table 16.4.

Dhrāana: Sixth Step of Hatha Yoga

According to Yoga Darshana (3, 1), concentration is to maintain the mind fixed on one object. The movements of the mind are stalled through the concentration.

Dhyāna: Seventh Step of Hatha Yoga

Contemplation (Dhyāna) or meditation is the state of mind which begins to flow around a single object without any outward notion. There are three kinds of contemplation; material, luminous, and subtle.

1) Sthula Dhyāna (Material contemplation) in which of the mind is concentrated on deity or the image of Guru
2) Jyotir- Dhyāna (Luminous contemplation): The mind is focused on the radiance of Nature.
3) Sukshma- Dhyāna (Subtle Contemplation): The mind is

concentrated on the Kundalini.

Samādhi: Eighth Step of Hatha Yoga

Identification with Supreme Reality (Samādhi): According to Yoga Darshana (3.3), Samādhi or identification is the object of contemplation in which one's own form is annihilated; where Ātmā and mind become one.

As per the Shiva Siddhanta, Samādhi liberates the self from the manifestations of cognitions. The Seer who attained this stage becomes insensible to heat or cold, to sorrow or pleasure. Yoga promises, in this form, the Yogi (Yogini) should be able to perceive the things of the past, present and future in this world and as well as other worlds in the other universes, even though earth-bound and belonging to a particular space-time coordinates. Probably, this is how the ancient Vedic Seers perceived the inter-galaxy travel.

One rarely attains this stage in one's life time, there are very few persons in the history who achieved liberation. The closest example is Sri Aurobindo Ghose who attained path of enlightenment (Samādhi) in 1926 and after that Sri Ghose went into seclusion and stopped talking to his disciples. Shri Ghose teachings focus on supreme realization through two-way path as given below.

1) Human beings possess "Spiritual Supermind", which enables them to reach upwards towards illumination.

2) The divinity up above is the source for enlightenment.

One attains spiritual perfection through Astanga Yoga that leads to the liberation through two-way path.

References (Sanskrit language):

- The Hatha-Yoga Pradipikā
- The Yoga Darshana (Patanjali)
- The Darshana Upanishad
- Yoga Kundalini Upanishad
- The Shiva Samhitā (Hatha Yoga and Raja Yoga)
- The Gorakshā Samhitā (Hatha Yoga by Gorakshā Nathā)
- The Gherandra Samhitā
- Sānkhya Pranchana (Commentary of Vyāsa)
- The Bhagavad Gitā (deals with Karma Yoga)
- The Bhāgavata Purāna (deals with Bhakti, Raja and Karma Yoga)
- Mārkandeya Purāna (deals with Mantra Yoga)

17. Perini Shiva Thandavam

The five senses are linked with five elements.
The five seasons are like the five breadths of the mind.
The five directions are the five organs of cognition controlled by the soul.
These organs are located in the head and connected with the soul.

(Atharva Veda 8.9.15)

Perini Dance

The **Perini Shiva Thandavam** is an ancient form of rigorous dance, dedicated to the Supreme dancer, Lord Shiva. Mainly performed by the male warriors before going to the war. The Shiva Thandavam dance was prevalent in Deccan during the Satavahana Dynasty, between 230 BCE and 230 CE, and it reached its pinnacle during the Kakatiya rule. The Kakatiya General Recherla Rudra during the reign of Kakatiya ruler Ganapati Deva, reinvented this Perini dance, as per the inscriptions written inside the 800-year-old Shiva temple located at, Palampet village, Warangal, Telangana, India.

Telangana is a new state situated in south central India, formerly part of erstwhile Andhra Pradesh. The word Telangana is derived from Sanskrit, which translates to the country of three Lingas. As per Hindu legend, Lord Shiva descended in the form of Shiva-Lingas on the three mountains **"Srishailam"**, **"Kaleshwaram"** and **"Draksharamam"**, which form the boundary of the **Trilingadesa**. The name of the Trilingadesa later changed to **Telangana** in 14th century AD.

Ramappa – A Master Piece of Architecture

The word "Perini" derived from the "Prerana" means inspiration in Telugu. The Perini dance almost disappeared after the demise of the Kakatiya dynasty. But the credit goes to **Padmasri Dr. Nataraja Rama Krishna** for bringing it back to alive on Feb 17, 1985. As a student, I had a privilege to witness this dance. The historical dance was performed at Ramappa gudi (temple), Palampet Village, Telangana on the occasion of Shivaratri festival. The Palampet village is located approximately 75 km from Warangal, an ancient capital of Kakatiya dynasty.

As per the local news more than 1.5 million people visited to witness the dance on that day. I went there along with my classmates by bus. Thousands of pilgrims blocked the whole area up to 15 kilometers away from the main Temple. So, we all started walking, after a while, I bumped into a Koyalu tribal priest (a pujari for forest Bhairava). Based on my conversation with the tribal priest, that day happened to be a special occasion. A rare Shivaratri day, which comes after every Six hundred years. I was about to ask which Calendar they follow, the priest disappeared into the forest. The tribal people probably use either Saptarishi or Julian (Jupitar based) calendar. Based on my research the year 1985 happens to be 9th such special occasion. Which confirms that the Shivaratri celebrated for more than 5400 years (since 3415 BCE) by the local people.

History of Ramappa

The Ramappa temple (named after the sculptor Ramappa) built in the year 1213 is an architectural Master piece. The temple foundation is built using red sand stone, an earth quake resistance construction, it's called "sandbox technology", the technology was unique to the Kakatiyas and couldn't be found anywhere else.

Illustration 17.1: Ramappa Temple, the main deity Shiva, built on Mach 31, 1213 AD (courtesy: ASI, Ramappa temple)

The evidence of the existence of Perini dance during the ancient times could be found based on the dancing poses shown on the sanctuary doorway carvings. It's located on a high Pedestal of black basalt rock. These are life size sculptors of tall, Nobel and Ferocious Dancing girls. They are carrying swords, bows and arrows. The names of female warriors in dance poses are Madabika, Nagini, Alasakanya and Salabhangika.

Pentathlon of Dance

The Perini Shivathandam has five Stages (Angas) of dance:

1. Ghargaram - The dance attempts to invoke Lord Shiva through 5 styles of leg moments.
2. Vishamam – Acrobatic dance poses to fire up the Kundalini

3. Bhavasharayam – Invoking Shiva through imitation of nature, animals and demons
4. Kaivaram - The praise of the great Kings and gods
5. Geetam – Dancing to the high tones of Music

Illustration 17.2: Ramappa Temple, the carvings depicting the Perini Dance poses (courtesy: ASI, Ramappa temple)

Illustration 17.3: Ramappa Temple, the life size sculptors of the tall, Nobel and Ferocious Dancing girls (courtesy: ASI, Ramappa temple)

The purpose of the dance is to elevate the spiritual levels of the warriors and fire up the Shasrara and Ajna Chakras as well as the third eye so that they can be alert from the enemy attacks from all sides. There are several historic places in the nearby cities such as Thousand pillar temple, Hanumakonda, Kakatiya Fort, etc. But, the Ramappa temple is not about the God or religion, it's about the ancient, most vigorous and physically challenging dance called Perini. It's like Triathlon of Olympics or Pentathlon of dance because of five stages of dance.

Section – V

(Definition of God)

18. What is God?

True definition of God

Is God transcendent, meaning above the world? Is God personal, can you have one-on-one? The world's oldest spiritual Tradition, also known as Hinduism, which evolved out of later Vedic and Puranic Traditions gives you the clear definition of God. In Hinduism, acknowledgement of people comes first, and their beliefs in existence of many gods - the divine beings who are avatars or manifestations of Brahman and their practices constitute the spiritual tradition. In Puranic or Late Vedic Traditions, God was defined as the ultimate truth or reality; the Brahman or Absolute and omnipresent reality pervading the Universe, which comes to us through personal experience of divine consciousness.

Lord Krishna, an original author of Bhagavad-Gita and king of mythical city Dwaraka - which was submerged into the sea more than five thousand years ago; identified himself as the reincarnation of Lord Vishnu. Lord Vishnu is the symbolic representation of Ananta or Infinite or Multiverse. The statue of Lord Vishnu and his incarnations always carved out of black stone, a symbolic representation of dark matter which binds together the whole universe. Bhagavad-Gita, meaning in Sanskrit "song of the Lord", reveals God as Omnipotent, Omnipresent and the only real actor in the universe who responds to the love of his devotees. After Bhakti movement (100CE – 900CE) in India, the Ishvara (Shiva or Krishna or the incarnations of Vishnu) is conceived as personal, the way of personal devotion. Even though majority of the Indian princely states were under foreign invasions and occupation for several centuries, the spirituality of Upanishads and the fervent Bhakti movement didn't die. Present day Hinduism is the continuation of the ancient Vedic civilization and Puranic Traditions. Hinduism is not a religious symbol, the Hindu tradition encourages individuals to seek truth-consciousness (moral and spiritual truth) through their own efforts, by whatever means and wherever it might be found. Whereas the scared Vedas and post-Vedic scriptures, Upanishads, Bhagavad-Gita, Ramayana, Mahabharata and Puranas serve as the reference books.

In many religions, truth is revealed to the world from a divine source through an agent (example - Abraham in Judaism, Muhammad in Islam, and Jesus in Christianity), so - an individual is expected to follow it as a divine truth. Goutham Buddha, the founder of Buddhism rejected the soul, but neither accepted nor rejected the God. Vardhamana Mahavira (539 BCE - 467 BCE), founder of Jainism rejected God but accepted Soul. In Biblical traditions (Christianity, Islam, Judaism), the God, conceived as the unity, transcendent and personal. The world has seen some great thinkers in the 6th Century BCE, such as Zoroaster, Heraclitus, Confucius and Lao Tse who opposed the orthodox system, but they all accepted God in one form or other. According to Hebrew scriptures the world is an emanation of God. Its forbidden to create any images of the God. The Christianity began as a Jewish Sect, in the beginning Old Testament as the divine source. By the end of 1st century CE, Christians had exalted Jesus as the holy man of God, which was a direct conflict with the Jewish concept of monotheism. Around 4th century CE, Christians came up with a solution "Trinity", based on the doctrine of trinitas, developed by Tertullian, a theologian in the 2nd century CE. According to this doctrine, the God exists as Father, Son and Holy Spirit, who are united as one being.

The Hindu concept of Trinity which was developed more than eight thousand years ago, around 6,000 BCE, identifies God with form of the scared syllable OM (pronounced as A-U-M). In other words, God can be identified in three cosmic states creation (Brahma), preservation (Vishnu) and dissolution (Shiva). With the polytheistic rhetoric, Rig Veda failed to provide the clear definition of God. But, later on one can find a clean solution to the God issue in both Agamas and Upanishads through a meta-physical connection, which is also called as Vedanga.

Based on the descriptions available in the later Vedic scriptures and Agamas, the "Pure Consciousness" is the closest definition of God. One might wonder, how to reach the state of Pure Consciousness? It might be impossible for the regular people to experience the Pure-consciousness unless they devote their entire life, just like a Himalayan Yogi, who attains the final stage of Astanga Yoga (refer to the chapter on Yoga Philosophy for more details). The regular folks might experience a stripped-down version of Truth-Consciousness, through various means such as the medium of bhakti or personal devotion, through singing or dancing or practicing Yoga & Meditation. Different People call the consciousness with different names, some people also call it as the Global or Infinite consciousness, others as Universal consciousness or External consciousness or Cosmic Knowledge etc.

One might question, what is the underlining purpose of me being born here on the planet Earth? If you listen to the late night radio shows such as George Noor's coast2coast AM, many people ask this kind of question, but there were no real answers. The plain and direct answer is …

"Unfortunately, there is no ready-made answer available. it's your job to find out yourself …"

The longer you live the probability of finding your purpose on the Earth improves. Believe it or not attaining Consciousness has the direct impact on one's longevity. So, its immaterial whether you are a believer in God or a non-believer, attaining Truth-Consciousness is the key survival technique. Till now, the modern science didn't find any solution to the phenomenon of pure-consciousness. So, the Vedas still remain the ultimate spiritual authority that permeates human thought process till the end of Kali Yuga.

An alternative definition of God

The alternative definition of God based on the concept of biological mechanism was first described in the Taittrīyā Upanishad (around 4,000 BCE) as follows:

"Mathru Devo Bhava   Pitru Devo Bhava"

The literal meaning of the "Mathru Devo Bhava Pitru Devo Bhava", the biological father and mother are the forms of the God. The Vedic Sages were probably aware of biological inheritance and similar type of DNA concept and therefore they tried to explain why the biological mother and father were the symbols of God. As per modern science, DNA (deoxyribonucleic acid) is a single molecule that passed on from parents to offspring that contains coded instructions just like machine language program used in computers, that enables to develop from a single cell into a full-blown adult body. Who knows what is inside this single cell other than what you could see under electron microscope? There may be billions and trillions of tiny ancient micro civilizations sitting inside a single cell and we probably have no means to find out about this with the technology available today. Who has the ability to code the DNA instructions? Other than the biological parents, nobody else could provide DNA instructions to their offspring and hence the Vedic Sages called the mother and father as the forms of the God. Let us assume AI (Artificial Intelligence) somehow gets the handle on DNA sequencing and an ability to reprogram biological instructions, then the terrible things might happen on the planet Earth such as re-birth of dinosaurs, the giraffe might give birth to cheetah instead of giraffe, etc., only time will tell how the AI going to transform the world?

Jayadeva - An Example of pure-consciousness

Jayadeva, a devotional 12th Century Sanskrit poet from Orissa, India. He wrote a lyrical epic called 'Gita Govinda'. It's a romantic story about the divine love of Lord Krishna and Gopika heroine Radha. The writer suffered from a mental block when he reached the critical stage of the poem. He took a break from the writing and decided to take bath in the river, Yamuna. As he bathed in the river, the divine power continued to wrote in his place[1]. How could it be possible unless you blindly believe in orthodox divine stories?

When Jayadeva took a bath in the river, he might have experienced truth-consciousness or 'Higher Order Thought'. Two Vedic gods involved in Jayadeva's river bath, Vayu and Indra. The Vedic God Indra, who is the life-giving Sun has a direct impact on the mental energies of a person. And another Vedic God Vayu (air) which is associated with Prana or nervous activity of a person. After experiencing the divine bliss (consciousness), it might have cleared the mental blocks, and Jayadeva could finish his literary work without any difficulty. The divine power of Lord Krishna is only a symbolism here. It's the divine bliss that enabled the Jayadeva to write (The scientific information about this phenomenon of chakras that triggers consciousness and the related chemicals, neurotransmitters, hormones, and amino acids etc., involved in this process given elsewhere in this book). Pretty much every human being has an ability to experience Consciousness just like Jaya Deva. This may be the reason why more than 100 million people take part in the Khumba Mela and Pushkaram that occur after every twelve years at Triveni Sangam, Allahabad, India.

19. Creation & Destruction

"Earnestness is the path to the Eternal. Thoughtlessness is the path to death. Those who are earnest will never die. Those who are thoughtless are as if dead already"

(Dhammapada, V.21.)

Gayatri Mantra

The "Gayatri Mantra" is one of the most powerful ancient Vedic hymns (Rigveda 3.62.10), which describes the creation and destruction as a cycle of on-going process.

"Om bhur bhuvah svaha
tat savitur vareneyam
bhargo devasya dhimahi
dhiyo to nah prachodayat"

Om! The primeval sound created by the rotation of

Sun, Earth, Moon, Navagraha, Nakshatra etc., at the beginning of Kalpa (when Universe born), signifying the presence of Supreme being, without this planetary motion the life won't exist. Our bodies made of Pancha Bhootas (five elements), these elements are Prithivi or Earth, Jal or Water, Agni or Fire, Vayu or Air, Aakas or Aether. Supreme being is the one gives life to all and alone can take away the life. The word "Bhuva" indicates Supreme being's role as the remover of suffering and pain. The "Savitur" signifies the Supreme Lord's ability to create Universe, sustain it, and bring about its dissolution. The Gayatri Mantra decimates ignorance, it illuminates intellect and produces the highest bliss, and creativity just like Sun liquidates the darkness.

Apart from the spiritual meaning, reciting Gayatri Mantra 108 times (20 Minutes a day) has a positive effect on human body because it enlightens the mind and improves the breathing and quality of speech. This ancient Vedic mantra was chanted for several thousands of years before it was revealed to the Brahmarshi Vishvamitra during the Treta Yuga.

Vedic concept of creation

As per Rig-Veda (verse 10.121.1), Prajapati (Brahmandam) is the creator of the Universe. Where did the creator come from? Even though there are some serious flaws around this theory, several ancient scriptures and Manu Smirti (Laws of Manu) supports this theory. Ancients were probably aware of this error and they later fixed it by introducing Lord Vishnu (see section on Puranic concept of creationism). In the beginning of Kalpa, the whole Universe was in the form of paramanu (sub-atomic particles), asat (state of non-being), dark, invisible and subtle substance. The Vedic philosophers (sages and Rishis) called it as Hiranyagarbha (Golden womb). The next step was generation of immense heat that contributed to formation Sun, earth, planets, stars etc.

The following is the Rigveda verse 10.121.1, the Sanskrit scripture that was composed around 13th century BCE, but the original hymns existed in oral form for more than eight thousand years before that.

हिरण्यगर्भः समवर्तताग्रे भूतस्य जातः पतिरेकासीत ।
स दाधार पृथ्वीं ध्यामुतेमां कस्मै देवायहविषा विधेम ॥

hiraṇyagarbhaḥ samavartatāgre
bhūtasya jātaḥ patirekāsīta /
sa dādhāra pṛthvīṃ dhyāmutemāṃ
kasmai devāyahaviṣā vidhema //

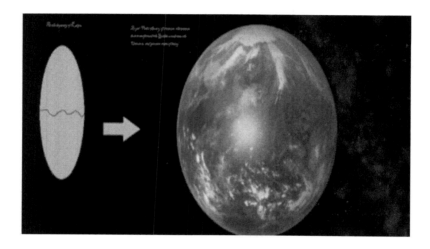

Illustration: 19.1: Vedic concept of Creationism, according to which the whole Universe was in the egg form made of paramanu (sub-atomic particles), asat (state of non-being), invisible dark energy and subtle substance.

The intense heat raised the paramanu to the state of self-luminous vapors, this has been called by the Vedic Sages as the Prajapati or Brahma (the lord of all creations). The transformation of asat (un-manifested) to sat (manifested) within the time-space parameters is the essence of the Vedic creation. The Big-Bang theory claims 14 billion years ago hot cosmic fire ball created the matter we see around us today, but it doesn't explain where did the fireball come from?

Biblical concept of creationism

As mentioned in Microsoft Encarta, Creationism is   the political movement of the United States right wing Judeo-Christian fundamentalists. Per which all the living beings were created by Intelligent Designer, God.   In contrast to the Darwin's theory of evolution. The creationists believe the entire Universe was created within the past Six thousand years. But, the scientific community believe the life itself arose from the blind and undirected physical process. This idea was widely opposed by the creationists.

Is creationism possible? There is nothing in the world that could prove that Creationism didn't occur. At the same time, there is no proof available to confirm that the life on the Earth started because of either Creationism or Darwin's theory of Evolution. So, it's hard to prove which one is correct, whether the world created because of creationism or by natural selection. This is always a fruitless argument just like theory of Geocentric versus Heliocentric. The DNA evidence suggests the theory of evolution based on Random Genetic Mutation (or Natural Selection) already started falling apart. So, people might re-consider Vedic creationism. For the sake of argument, let us assume that there is an intelligent designer or eternal God sitting elsewhere in the Universe. It's still not clear, how a single God can handle billions of lives? May be the creationists should come up with a theory that the god is talking through his human manifestations or Avatars? In June, 2006, more than 100 scientists and Professors from various Universities around the globe published a Scientific Dissent from Darwinism as given below:

"We are skeptical of claims for the ability of random mutation and natural selection to account for the complexity of Life. Careful examination of the evidence for Darwinian theory should be encouraged."

Puranic Concept of Creationism

As per the Puranas, the Lord Brahma created life on the planet Earth. Lord Brahma is a mythical character in the Puranas, it represents the Brahmandam or the Universe. It's a combination of theory of evolution and the Biblical theory of Creationism. The only thing, the Puranic concept was developed at least six thousand years before the birth of

Christ. There might be a question where did Lord Brahma come from? To fix this, the Sages came up with another deity. Lord Vishnu, who represents the creator of Ananta (infinite or multiverse) as shown in the illustration 19.2.

The name Lord Vishnu derived from the name of the Dravidian astronomer who might have lived sometime between 24,000 BCE and 17,000 BCE. He was the first Astronomer to come up with Nakshatra system based on the astronomical references found in the Vedic texts. There might be another question how does the Lord Vishnu know when to create a Universe? So, the Ancient Indian Rishis came up with another philosophical thought known as Avatars. They initially wanted to create 16 avatars but it's now restricted to Ten (as described in the Chapter 7 - Supreme God Vishnu). This way Lord Vishnu keeps in touch with each and every Universe he creates through his Avatars. Based on this concept Ancient Indian Astronomers accurately calculated the life of the Universe several thousands of years ago, which is pretty close to the modern scientific estimation.

The symbolism of the Lord Vishnu is Ananta (endless or infinite of universes or Multiverse) and the life is propagated from outer space into each Universe when it was created. Within the Universe the life seeds propagated through Meteors or Comets or some flying objects, which is equivalent to the Lord Brahma creating the life on Earth. The Avatars represent the theory of evolution. The first avatar started with fish (lives only in the water); second avatar - Turtle (which can live on Earth as well as water); third avatar - Varaha (wild boar, which can live on the earth); the fourth avatar - Narasimha, an anthropomorphic form of Human body with lion's head and claws; the fifth avatar - a human but in a dwarf shape; the sixth avatar - the Parushurama, a human warrior and the remaining three avatars (Sri Rama, Lord Krishna, Goutham Buddha) all in the human form as well. It's beyond anybody's imagination how the Ancient Indian Puranic Sages could accurately predict the human evolution. What about the 10th Avatar Kalki? The ancient Indian Sages predicted that this avatar will bring an end to the life on Earth for any number of reasons. So, it's not just man-made atmospheric pollution or Global Warming that's an immediate threat to the world, but anything from Solar flares to AI (Artificial Intelligence) enabled humanoid robots or Extra Terrestrial invaders who might end the human civilization here on Earth.

Illustration 19.2: Lord Ananta (Lord Vishnu – symbolism for Multiverse) in Yoga Nidra (sleeping on cosmic snake). Brahma sprouts out of his naval is the Symbolism of the Universe (Acknowledged to: Vishnu's Anantasayana, Paining Kangara, Himachal Pradesh, 18th Century CE)

20. Theory of Reincarnation

Earth, water, fire, air, ether, thought, reasoning, and consciousness of an individuality - these are eight-fold divisions of my nature.

-Bhagvad Gita (VII-4)

(Arjuna was reluctant to fight against his cousins and relatives, Lord Krishna revealed himself to Arjuna as a reincarnation of Supreme God Vishnu and taught him Bhagvad Gita in the battle field of Kurukshetra and later served as his charioteer and helped him win the Mahabharata war)

Reincarnation a myth or reality?

Is reincarnation a myth or reality? Ancient Indians always believed in reincarnation of a soul, which occurs as per the Karmas did in the past life. Karma means either good or bad actions carried out when a person is alive as described in the Upanishads, sacred Vedic scriptures. Ancient Hindus strongly believed that the only solution to liberate from millions of cycles of re-birth is by attaining Moksha at the 3500-year old holy city of Varanasi. According to the Vedic traditions, a person gets Moksha if cremated after the death in this holy city. As per the legend, even if the person is cremated elsewhere, by merging ashes in the Ganga river by his family members at Varanasi gets an instant gateway to Heaven and relieved from the burden of infinite cycles of re-birth (Illustration 20.2).

Theory of Reincarnation

The theory I am going to explain is based on the ancient Indian belief, the Karma Siddhanta.

"The re-incarnation possible only if the body is cremated after the death, and the ashes were scattered in the river for energy re-cycling. The belief that the soul is eternal is just an orthodox sentiment. And it doesn't collaborate with the historical or scientific facts."

For example, the molecules inside the ashes merged in the river Ganges (Illustration 20.2) after cremation goes through the energy re-cycling and it has a pretty good chances of going through re-incarnation process. The people of Ancient Indian have been doing this for several thousands of years, since beginning of the time. So, there is no guaranty that reincarnation could happen if the body is buried instead of cremated.

Illustration 20.1: Night view of the most spectacular Ganga Ghat (also known as Dashashwamedh ghat), Varanasi, a major pilgrimage spot where Ganga Aarti is performed daily in the evening. This mystical tradition has been taking place uninterrupted for more than 3500 years.

Illustration 20.2: It's a 4,000-year-old Vedic tradition; Hindus believe that if the ashes of the deceased are laid in the Ganges at Varanasi, the soul gets an instant gateway to Heaven and attains Moksha.

After cremation the ashes merged in the ganga river at Banaras and it eventually ends up in the ocean

Re-birth occurs due to the energy re-cycling

Illustration 20.3: Cycle of reincarnation or Energy re-cycling.

Meta-physics of Reincarnation

Indian mythology always talk about the Ayodhya prince Lord Rama who was born in the Treta yuga (some 9000 years ago, from present time) as the avatar of Lord Vishnu. He believed to have been re-incarnated as the Lord Krishna in the Dwapara yuga. There are several incidents where people claimed that they could remember certain incidents from the previous births. These stories about rebirth can neither be verified nor be treated as false entities. The purpose of this chapter is to explain the theory behind this kind of phenomenon. The Illustration 20.3 explains the re-incarnation theory based on the energy re-cycling that has been taking place in ancient India for the last several thousands of years.

The human life on planet Earth is filled with both sorrows and pleasures. The Vedanta explains that the reincarnation happens at the meta-physical level based on the Karma (or Gunas). It's just an effort to reward the person when he dies based on his Character. It's a very powerful philosophical thought which forces everyone to do good things while they are alive, an effort to improve the human protocol and reduce the crime. Other than the meta-physical re-incarnation philosophical thought, is there any scientific evidence available at this point of time to prove the theory? Majority of the Indians even though they may not believe in God or in the Orthodox Karma Siddhanta, but they still worship the God and follow the Karma Siddhanta principles as a tradition rather than orthodox religious belief.

Lord Krishna was the king of the mythical city Dwaraka assumed to be the 8th reincarnation of god Vishnu. The Dwaraka city no longer exists today. Its presumably submerged in to the gulf of Cambay several thousands of years ago. The marine archeologists recently found the remains of the legendary lost city under the sea. Which suggests that the Lord Krishna's Dwaraka is no longer a mythical city but a genuine historical account.

As per the legend, the Dwaraka did exist five thousand years ago, and the city was completely submerged into the sea after the war between Lord Krishna and Salva. Mahabharata describes the King Salva attacked Dwaraka with a sophisticated flying machine when Lord

Krishna was away from the city. By the time, Lord Krishna came back it was too late and the city started submerging into the sea due to plate tectonic activity. Lord Krishna counter attacked Salva with his weapons and later killed him in the war. The Lord Rama born to kill the evil demons and Lord Krishna born to eradicate evil kingdoms. Is the reincarnation just a philosophical thought? If not, are there any biological facts associated with this? The reincarnation is another method through which animal world connected to the Gods. As per the Indian Mythology, when Lord Vishnu lied upon the cosmic snake Adi-Shesha, its reincarnated as the Balarama, Krishna's brother. There is no symbolism here, other than the story telling skills of Rishis of ancient India. They came up with the meta-physical relationship between the pets and gods through reincarnation. The reincarnation is nothing but honoring or elevating the state of a dead person or animal.

Egyptian Transmigration

Egyptians always believed in Transmigration; which appears to be like ancient Indian form of reincarnation but there are subtle differences. Transmigration is passing of soul at the death into a new form of being or new body. The Ancient Egyptians believed that the entombment (the mummified bodies) of the royals inside the pyramids would ensure that the souls live forever. The Large Pyramids were built in Egypt to protect the tombs.

As shown in Illustration 20.4, the Kings chamber located at the upper level. The queens chamber at the middle level and the bottom chamber where used to store gold and treasures. As per the legend, Asura architect Maya built the Pyramids of Giza somewhere around 2600 BCE. The Maya is not a person but a tribe, probably belongs to the same lineage of Aztecs of Mexico and Mayans of South America. The Mayas are the wondering tribe, they built several Palaces and rock caves in

Ancient India, including the palace of Pandavas, "Maya Shaba", which they built around 3150 BCE.

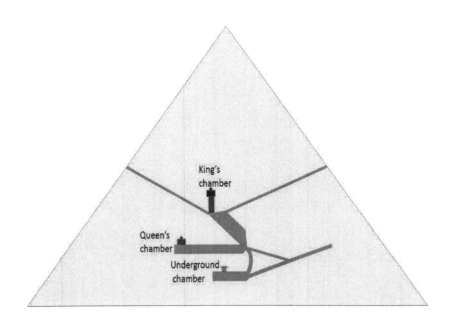

Illustration 20.4: The burial Chambers inside an Egyptian Pyramid

Concluding Remarks

If at all any sort of re-incarnation exists, it's just the energy re-cycling after death (see the Illustration 20.3). Other than that, the existence of soul and passing from one body to another or from one dimension to another dimension can't be proven at this point of time. The soul concept mentioned in Upanishads and Bhagvad Gita was to counsel grieving loved ones of a deceased person or animal and at the same time rewarding the people based on their Gunas or good deeds. As described in the ancient Vedic scriptures, the relationship between mind and body is considered as the "Soul" (mentioned in Katha Upanishad III. 10-12). People are expected to concentrate all their thoughts on the inner guide or soul as well as observe the outer world through their internal senses in order to attain the truth-consciousness.

During the Vedic times, the constellations in the Northern Hemisphere were considered as the heaven, whereas the Asterisms in the southern hemisphere as the hell. Some people may believe in after death experience with bright lights, but it's an individual choice if the person wants to believe in it or not. In other words, the concept of God, Divinity and Re-incarnation are the personal choices, therefore live and let live is the best policy. Never ending struggle of the humanity is to synchronize the God within your mind (Truth-Consciousness) with the Universal God (Infinite-Consciousness) up above to reap the benefits of increased mental, physical and emotional stability. Practicing Yoga is a proven spiritual method that helps an individual to align the Body and Mind with the Pancha Bhootas (five elements surrounding you - Prithivi or Earth, Jal or Water, Agni or Fire, Vayu or Air, Aakas or Aether) in order to attain truth-consciousness and longevity.

Key to Sanskrit Pronunciation

ā	as in father
ś	as in Supervision
ī	as in Sweet
ū	as in Soothe

Appendix-I

Research studies on Ancient Vedic history shows, there was no segregation of women in Vedic civilization. The daughters and wives of Vedic Sages had an ample opportunity to learn and contribute towards the development of ancient societies.

The Women Vedic Seers

Name	Vedic Family
Viswavarā	School of Atri (Rig Veda V.28.0 III 4.3)
Apālā	Daughter of Sage Atri (Rig Veda VIII 91.1 – 91.7)
Sasvatī	Daughter of Sage Angirasa (Rig VIII)
Lopāmudra	Wife of Sage Agastya (Rig X.125.1-8)
Savitri	Rig X.85
Atreyi	Rig V.28

The South Indian Vedic Seers

Given below is the list of Vedic Seers from Deccan and Southern India, who participated in the compilation of Rig-Veda to the modern Sanskrit format. They originally inherited Vedas from their ancestors in the oral format, but composed in some kind of extinct languages such as ancient Dravidian or ancient Sanskrit.

Vishwamitra School (Owner of Mandala 3)

1.   Kaushika
2.   Gathi
3.   Rishabha
4.   Devavat
5.   Vaishvamitra (Shunas-Shepa Ajigarti)

Bhardwaj School (Owner of Mandala 2)
1. Angirasa
2. Deerghatamas
3. Brhaspata Bhardwaja

Kanva School (Owner of Mandala 8)
1. Ghora
2. Medhatithi
3. Pragaatha
4. Bharga
5. Kali
6. Haryaat
7. Saubhari
8. Gautama
9. Raahugana
10. Bhargava Jamadagni
11. Garga
12. Payu

Atri School (Owner of Mandala 5)
1. Bhauma
2. Bhudha
3. Isha
4. Gaya
5. Sootambhara
6. Sasa
7. Aarchanaanasa
8. Paura
9. Awaasyu
10. Shatahavya
11. Uru Chakri
12. Swati
13. Pratiratha
14. Babhru
15. Gaatu
16. Poetesses Apaala
17. Vishvavaaraa

Angiras & Goutama school (Owners of Mandala 6, 1 & 4)
1. Khutsa
2. Viroopa
3. Gopavana

Others:
1. Kavasha Ailusha
2. Samvannana

Appendix -II

Ancient Universities in India (600 BCE to 1000 CE)

Indian sub-continent is the place where most of the ancient Universities or ancient seat of learning can be found. It wouldn't be exaggerated to say that the modern science & medicine might not even existed today without the contributions from the Ancient Universities such as Nagarjunakonda University, Takshasilā, Nalanda University, Odantapuri, Somapura, Jagaddala, Vallabhi, Vikrama Sila etc.

Nagarjunakonda: The Nagarjunakonda University in the Deccan area, old name Sriparvata, flourished from 12th century BCE to 3rd CE, attracted more than 10,000 students from all over the world, highly specialized in Medicine, Surgery, ophthalmology, fine arts, Astronomy, Mahayana Buddhist philosophy, Agriculture and Mathematics, Metallurgy and Chemistry. The University received endowment from more than 100 surrounding villages.

Nalanda: The Nalanda University flourished during the period 5th Century BCE to 12th Century CE. There were 1,510 teachers and it attracted 8,500 students from around the world. It was popular for Architecture, Astronomy, Mathematics, Metallurgy, Structural and Marine Engineering, Chemistry, Vedas, Arts, Astronomy and warfare & Defense Studies, Economics, Literature and Buddhist studies. Nagarjuna, a famous Buddhist Philosopher, who founded Madhyamika school of Mahayana Buddhism was the faculty member of University of Nalanda during 3rd Century CE.

Takshasilā: The Takshasilā, the capital of ancient Gandhara in the northwest of the Indian Subcontinent (Present day Pakistan) was an important ancient seat of learning (1000 BCE – 500 CE) as well as the ancient trade centre (for Silk, Cotton, Sandalwood and diamonds) during the Kushan period (1ˢᵗ Century CE to 5ᵗʰ Century CE). Per the puranic records, the Takshasilā was the great centre for learning Buddhist Sutras, Ayurvedic Medicine, Vedas, Economics, Alchemy, Archery, Hunting and Battleground skills.

Illustration II.1: Ruins of Nalanda University (500BCE – 1200 CE)

Illustration II.2: Ruins of Takshasilā University (1000 BCE – 500 CE)

Copyright Acknowledgements

References

1. The Holy Vedas a Golden Treasury, Pandit Satykam Vidyalankar, 1983, Clarion Books

2. The Secret of the Veda, Sri Aurobindo, 1987, Fifth Impression, Sri Aurobindo Ashram Pondicherry

3. Rgvedic Legends - through the ages, H.L. Hariyappa, 1953

4. Wastav Ramayanam, P.V. Vartak

5. The Hindus – an alternative History, Wendey Doniger, 2009, Penguin Group

6. India – a sacred Geography, Diana Eck, 2012, Harmony Brooks

7. Dancing with Siva – Hinduism's Contemporary Catechism, 1993, Himalayan Academy

8. Advancements of Ancient India's Vedic culture, Stephen Knapp, 2012

9. Llewellyn Complete Book of Chakras, Cyndi Dale, 2016, First Edition, Llewellyn Publications, MN

10. The Jaiminigrhyasūtra, W. Caland, 1984, Motilal Banarsidass

11. Hinduism, A short Summary, Klaus K. Klostermaier, 2000, One World Publications

12. Indian Journal of History of science, 28(1), 1993, A search for the Earliest Vedic calendar

13. In Search of the Cradle of Civilization – New Light on Ancient India, Georg Feuerstein, Subash Kak, and David Frawly

14. Microsoft Encarta, Encyclopedia standard 2005

15. YOGA – The method of Re-Integration, 1949, Alain Danielou (Shiva Sharan), Christopher Johnson

16. The Historic Rama, Indian Civilization at the end of Pleistocene, Nilesh Nilkanth Oak, 2014

17. The Art and Science of Raja Yoga, Swami Kriyananda, 2002, Crystal Clarity Publishers

18. The Astronomical Code of Rgveda, Subhash Kak, 2011

References to Chapter-19:

[1] The biography of Adam von Trott a Good German – Giles MacDonogh

[2] Microsoft Encarta Encyclopedia Standard - 2005

[3] Third Reich, Christopher Ailsby, 2001

[4] The Holocaust in History, Michael R. Marrus, 1987, University Press

[5] War & Genocide – A Concise History of the Holocaust – Doris L. Bergen, 2009

Notes

Introduction

1.   Voyager 4.5 Dynamic Simulator; www.carinasoft.com
2.   Integrated History of Ancient India, 1994, author: L.S. Wakankar, p. 25
3.   History of Indian Science, Dr. P. Priyadarshi, MBBS, MD, FRCP(UK); p. 120
4.   B.G. Tilak, an author of the book published in 1893 CE, "The Orion, The Antiquity of the Vedas"
5.   Ancient Indian History (Telugu Translation), Hyderabad book Trust, 1983, written by Romila Thaper, p. 18
6.   Integrated History of Ancient India, 1994, author: L.S. Wakankar, p. 36
7.   In Search of the Cradle of Civilization – New Light on Ancient India, Georg Feuerstein, Subhash Kak, and David Frawly; p. xvi
8.   In Search of the Cradle of Civilization – New Light on Ancient India, Georg Feuerstein, Subhash Kak, and David Frawly; p.71
9.   Astronomical dating of the Ramayan, Dr. P.V. Vartak
10. History of Sangam Period, Thiru Chidambaranar, p. 24-29
11. Advancements of Ancient India's Vedic culture, Stephen Knapp, 2012; p. 18
12. Dancing with Shiva, Hinduisms Contemporary Catechism, Satguru Sivaya Subramuniyaswami, p. 611
13. Integrated History of Ancient India, 1994, author: L.S. Wakankar, p. 16
14. History of Sangam Period, Thiru Chidambaranar, p. 24-29
15. The Dawn of Indian Civilization, part-1, edited by G.C. Pande, ICPR, 2000, pp. 507-524; Astronomy and Its Role in Vedic Culture, Subhash Kak, p. 30
16. Based on the research conducted by Malti Shndge of Pune, Maharashtra, India; Sumerian and Akkadian languages of Mesopotamia are the offshoots of Sanskrit language because of its close affinity.

Based on the paper published by Prof. K.D. Abhyankar, Indian National Science Academy (INSA), Hyderabad, Telangana, India, the Parsis of Arianavayo (presumed an earlier home of Aryans) talk about the mystic river goddess Saraswati and whereas Vedas don't talk about Aryans, which prove that Indo-Aryans migrated out of India.
17.

What is God?

1.   India - people, place, culture, history; Abraham Eraly, & others. 2008; p. 265

Vedic Calendar

1.   A Search for The Earliest Vedic Calendar, K.D. Abhyankar, Indian Journal of History of Science, 28(1), 1993
2.   The Indian Journal of History of Science, December 2011, vol.46.4 (2011), p. 573-610
3.   A Genuine Approach to the study of Ancient Indian Science, Prof. K.D. Abhyankar, Fellow, Indian National Science Academy, Hyderabad, India
4.   Fundamentals of Nakshatra Astrology, MK Viswanath, Nairs Publishing House, Hyderabad, India (2013), p. 10
5.   A Search for The Earliest Vedic Calendar, K.D. Abhyankar, 1993; p. 5.

Date of Mahabharata War

1   Kurukshetra, P. Raja Gopala Naidu (Telugu), page 23
2   Jyotirvidabharna, Kalidasa (Chapter-X; verse-109)
3   Kota Venkata Chelam and some other scholars used 634 instead of 633 (because temple was built in 634 CE) for calculation purposes;

But this is incorrect because there is no 0 CE (AD) or 0 BCE (BC); therefore, it should be 633 years. Similarly, scholars added 37 years between Mahabharata and beginning of Kaliyuga, but it should be 36 years as defined in the Puranas.

Goddess Sarasvati
1. The dates are based astronomical dating by several scholars and archeological evidence such as AIHOLE inscription.
2. Integrated History of Ancient India, L.S. Wakankar, p. 48
3. Rgvedic Legends - through the ages, H.L. Hariyappa; p. 156

A New Theory – On Aryan Origins
1. Journal Human Genetics, Sharma, S .et al, 2009; p. 47-55

Supreme God Vishnu
1. Complete Book of Chakras, First Edition, 2016, Cyndi Dale, page 16
2. Complete Book of Chakras, First Edition, 2016, Cyndi Dale, page 169
3. You Staying you - The owner's Manual for Extending Your Warranty, written by Mehmet C. Oz, Michael F. Roizen and others; p. 184
4. Science Direct, October 2003, vol 40(2); Glial cells and Neurotransmission, p. 389 – 400
5. Studies in Hinduism, René Guénon, 2004, Sophia Perennis, p. 73.

Narakasura – The Demon of Darkness
1. The inner Journey – views from the Hindu Tradition; Parabola Anthology Series – 2009; p. 229
2. Shrimad Bhagavata by Krshna-Dwaipayana Vyasa, International Gita Society
3.
4. Microsoft Encarta Encyclopedia-2005; topic: Ramanuja

Jesus Christ - The Incarnate Son of God
1. The Biology of Kundalini, Jane Dixon, p.21
2. Killing Jesus, Bill O'Reilly & Martin Dugard, 2013, Henry Holt & Co.

Mahishasura Mardini
1. The Origin of the Indo-European Races and Peoples, V. Chockalingam Pillai, Chapter-I, p. 44

Creation & Destruction
1. Search on the YouTube for "Gayatri Mantra by Anuradha & Kavita Paudwal or Suresh Wadkar".

Hatha Yoga
1. YOGA – The method of Re-Integration, 1949, Alain Danielou (Shiva Sharan), Christopher Johnson
2. Hatha Yoga Pradipika, Yogi Svatmarama; translated by Pancham Sinh

Glossary

Agamas	Post-Sangam Sruti - Shaiva Siddhanta.
ART	assisted reproductive technology
Bhang	an edible preparation of cannabis used by the tribal people of India, this has been in use since the beginning of the time. The Vedas refer to Amrita, which is nothing but the some-wine mixed Bhang.
Brahman	Not priest, The Absolute and omnipresent reality conceived as pervading the Universe
Brahmin	Vedic Pundit - who is well versed in Vedas and Jyothisyam, who writes Janma Pathrika (birth charts based on Astigmatism) and performs Special pujas and Yagna at homes and Laxmi Pujas at Business establishments. In south central India, they are different from the priests (Ayavarulu) who perform puja at Temples.
Buddha	An enlightened guru; the teacher.
Chakravarty	an Emperor; it's not wheel spinning monarch as presumed by some of the western authors
Chatta	A Rice measurement used in the rural India, approximate weight 10 Kgs.
Daivajnas	The people involved in the temple works such as astrologers, priests etc.
Dhaniya	Cilantro
Dharitri	Earth (meaning in Sanskrit)
Divya Astras	Ancient chemical and atomic weapons developed by the Deccan & Himalayan Sages and Ancient Universities.
Equinox	The day on which night and day are equal in length. For people living Northern Hemisphere March 21 is the spring equinox and September 23 is the autumnal equinox or the beginning of autumn.
Gotra	Gotra is one of the most sophisticated genetic code developed by the ancient Hindus. The people belong to a particular gotra and same caste are expected to have

	the same paternal DNA lineage and therefore are not allowed to marry within the same Gotra.
Haldee	Turmeric
ippa	It's a Soma tree, botanical name Bassia Longifolia and binomial name - Madhuca Longifolia. The ippa (same as Vippa) is a tree grown in Telangana and parts of Southern India, the fruits resemble like white grapes from which the Soma wine is extracted. It's called Amrita if Soma is mixed with the Bhang.
IVC	Indus Valley Civilization
IVF technology.	In Vitro Fertilization, an assisted reproductive
Jaiminigrhyasūtra	The Jaimini School of Sama Veda
Jnanam	Three-fold scheme of Hindu Philosophy; Jnan – Knowledge, Bhakti – devotion, and Karma – duty
Jyothisya	Vedic Astrology
Jyothisyam	Jyothisya, Vedic Astrology which includes Vastu, Ayurveda and Panchangam (Vedic Astronomy).
Kshatriyas	Ruling class, original owners of Vedas before the arrival of Aryans.
Khumba Mela	The plate Tectonic activity changed the course of river Sarasvatī and merged it into the Yamuna. The sacred river Sarasvatī eventually dried up. To remember this event, Indian Emperor Harsha started the Hindus gathering at Prayag (Allahabad, Uttar Pradesh, India) every 12 years for a holy bath at a place where Yamuna, Sarasvatī (Hidden into Yamuna) and Ganga Merge. More than 100 Million Hindus take a holy dip to clean up all the sins, the biggest peaceful gathering of its kind in the world.
Mahākāntāra	the great forest that separates Deccan and north India
Moksha	Salvation from cycles of re-birth, ancient Hindu belief.
SWE	sex with eros
Sage	Vedic seer and profoundly wise person; a powerful metaphor for demi-gods
Solstice	The day on which Sun is either furthest from North or South based on where you live. In the Northern

Hemisphere, June 21 is the day when the Sun is furthest from north and the length of the time between Sunrise and Sunset is longest of the year, so it's called as the Summer Solstice. If you live in the Southern Hemisphere, the summer solstice falls on December 22. Similarly, the winter solstice or the first day of winter occurs on December 22 in the Northern hemisphere. On this day the Sun is located furthest from south and the duration between Sunrise and Sunset is the shortest in a year. In Southern Hemisphere, the summer solstice occurs on June 21.

Soma	The Soma drink was the most important aspect of the Vedic rituals, the juice extracted from Vippa Chettu milky white fruits resemble like moon.
Tithi	same as Thithi.
Thithi	A lunar day; the length varies from 19 hours to 26 hours based on the time it takes to increase the longitudinal angle between the Moon and the Sun to increase by 12°(degrees).
Triveni Sangam	A place where three rivers (Ganga, Yamuna and invisible river Sarasvatī) merge, near Allahabad, Uttar Pradesh, India.
Uttarayanam	Marks the beginning of the Sun's movement northward for six months' period.
Varsha	A year in Vedic Calendar.
Vippa	same as ippa
Yamapuri	Hypothetical adobe of Yama (God of Death)

About the Author

L. H. Reddy (Lingannagari, Hanmanth Reddy) is an Engineer, and has masters in Digital Systems and Computer Engineering and Bachelor's degree in Electronics and Instrumentation Engineering with several years of experience in VLSI design, Systems Modelling, ASIC and System-On-Chip (SOC) design and development at Major Indian and United States Fortune-500 corporations. And, also involved in Geo-physical exploration projects in early 1990s at a major public sector undertaking in India, during that time worked with a team of Geologists, Geo-physicists, Hydro-Geologists and Paleontologists. Apart from SOC & Embedded design, also interested in Ancient History, Archeology, Astrophysics, Etymology and Genetic Engineering. If you have any questions or suggestions, please email at: **lhreddy@live.com**.

Index

-END-

(Photo credit: India Posts, Ministry of Communications, Govt. of India)

31288867R00175

Printed in Great Britain
by Amazon